"Every member of every church board should read *High-Impact Church Boards*. T. J. Addington tells it like it is and provides valuable insight to help church boards get past the garbage that so easily ensnares them. The reality is, every church board has an 'impact' on their church; this book can help make the impact a positive one."

—JIM SEYBERT, consulting futurist, member of board,
Grace Bible Church, Arroyo Grande, California

"Regardless of context or ministry style, an increasing number of church leaders are asking how they can best organize to embody Christ in their community and get on with His mission. T. J. Addington has years of experience and a proven track record of guiding congregations into a satisfying answer to this potentially fractious question. *High-Impact Church Boards* clearly and crisply outlines a biblically sound strategy of church governance that works. I consider the book a strategic addition to a church leader's 'must have' library of church health resources. Buy a copy of *High-Impact Church Boards* for every member of your oversight team and then work and pray through it together."

—JIM FANN, church health director, EFCA

"This book should be required reading for all church leadership boards. T. J.'s ability to cross over the issues of varying structures to provide timeless and practical concepts, strategies, and methods is second to none. The church often finds itself in an identity crisis with regard to how things should be done, what is most important, and who is in charge, most of which can be traced back to the church boardroom and its members. *High-Impact Church Boards* will start a movement in your leadership that will bring focus and equip change while providing applicable practices that will pave the way for greater kingdom impact. The church needs this book!"

—MARK STEVENSON, managing director,
People Management International Inc.

"The insights from *High-Impact Church Boards* have helped our elders see the unhealthy behaviors and practices that had been dividing the board for years. With the help of T. J. Addington, we have developed and are now implementing a strategy for change. This will enable us to make a significant impact for Christ and His kingdom. I highly recommend this book for all church leadership boards, no matter how healthy they think they might be."

—DAVID DONLE, elder, Grace Community Bible Church, Fort Worth, Texas

"Somebody once quipped, 'When the horse is dead, dismount.' Too many committed leaders and talented pastoral staff are spending far too much time in committee meetings and board meetings that are either dead or dying a slow death. Quit complaining and do something about it. Reading *High-Impact Church Boards* as a team will help you dismount a dead system and get on the solution side of church polity nightmares. The stakes are too high. The world needs to hear the message of the gospel from healthy churches not hindered by conflict over the latest bylaws changes. Shame on us for replacing the New Testament with Robert's Rules of Order. Dismount!"

— CHRIS DOLSON, senior pastor, Blackhawk Church, Verona, Wisconsin

"I have come to realize that no group has greater impact on church's vitality or my own personal sense of fulfillment than the church board. Thanks, T .J., for this labor of love. We will put *High-Impact Church Boards* to work as a catalyst to maximize our leadership at Two Rivers Church!"

— BRAD BRINSON, senior pastor, Two Rivers Church, Knoxville, Tennessee

"If you would like to break and bridge the apparent impasse between pastor-led versus board-led models of church ministry, I heartily recommend reading *High-Impact Church Boards*. T. J. brings mature experience from counseling churches across varied organizational cultures to foster healthy thinking and implementation of processes by which the bride of Christ that God has placed in the sphere of your board service will 'build itself up in love' (Ephesians 4:16)."

— RAMESH RICHARD, PhD, ThD, professor, Dallas Theological Seminary; president, RREACH International

"*High-Impact Church Boards* is one of those books that will mark your life and create intentional change that will shape your ministry. T. J. Addington has poured his life experience in the field of worldwide church leadership into this book so that God's kingdom can move forward in a healthy way. This is a great book to consult as a guide and to use as a textbook for today's leaders who long for such valuable insights to assess their present situation and pave the way for healthy changes tomorrow."

— JOSEPH NAJEM, pastor, Evangelical Free Church, Beirut, Lebanon

"*High-Impact Church Boards* is a must-read for anyone serving the local church. T. J. Addington clearly explains how leaders, board members, and pastors can work together more effectively and build a culture and a team that can be used by God to impact their community and city. This book is a wonderful blend of biblical principles, years of experience, and expertise that is actionable, understandable, and believable. T. J. has made a significant contribution to the church."

— KEN LARSON, CEO and founder, Slumberland Furniture

"Wow, what an excellent resource for the challenges and opportunities that exist in ministry work! I believe that this tool will unleash healthy, unified organizations and leaders to make huge kingdom impact."

— MARK BANKORD, founder and directional leader, Heartland Community Church, Rockford, Illinois

T. J. ADDINGTON

HIGH
IMPACT
CHURCH
BOARDS

How to Develop
Healthy, Intentional, and Empowered
Church Leaders

NAVPRESS

NAVPRESS⬤

NavPress is the publishing ministry of The Navigators, an international Christian organization and leader in personal spiritual development. NavPress is committed to helping people grow spiritually and enjoy lives of meaning and hope through personal and group resources that are biblically rooted, culturally relevant, and highly practical.

For a free catalog go to www.NavPress.com
or call 1.800.366.7788 in the United States or 1.800.839.4769 in Canada.

© 2010 by T. J. Addington

All rights reserved. No part of this publication may be reproduced in any form without written permission from NavPress, P.O. Box 35001, Colorado Springs, CO 80935. www.navpress.com

NAVPRESS and the NAVPRESS logo are registered trademarks of NavPress. Absence of * in connection with marks of NavPress or other parties does not indicate an absence of registration of those marks.

ISBN-13: 978-1-60006-674-0

Cover design by Arvid Wallen
Cover image by Shutterstock

Some of the anecdotal illustrations in this book are true to life and are included with the permission of the persons involved. All other illustrations are composites of real situations, and any resemblance to people living or dead is coincidental.

All Scripture quotations in this publication are taken from the *Holy Bible, New International Version*® (NIV®). Copyright © 1973, 1978, 1984 by International Bible Society. Used by permission of Zondervan. All rights reserved.

Library of Congress Cataloging-in-Publication Data
Addington, T. J.
  High-impact church boards : how to develop healthy, intentional, and empowered church leaders / T.J. Addington.
    p. cm.
  Includes bibliographical references (p.   ).
  ISBN 978-1-60006-674-0
  1. Church officers. 2. Church committees. 3. Christian leadership.
I. Title.
  BV705.A27 2010
  262'.22--dc22

                                    2009039806

Printed in the United States of America

1 2 3 4 5 6 7 8 / 14 13 12 11 10

This book is dedicated to my mother and father,
who instilled in me a deep love for God's church;
to Mary Ann, my bride, who has paid the price
of my leadership without complaint;
and to Jon and Steve, my beloved sons,
who were always gracious in their father's absence.

And finally, to each of those with whom I have served
in church leadership.
You know who you are, and you are loved.

CONTENTS

PREFACE

High-Impact Church Boards comes from my experience of serving in local church leadership since my late teens — as a committee member, board member, board chair, pastor, and, for many years now, consultant. While I love the church, it deeply frustrates me when we allow poor practices to muddle our ministries.

This book is a labor of love for all church leaders who long for better results from their leadership. It's written to encourage those brave souls who, in spite of the challenges and discouragements, have answered God's call to lead His church. It's written to remind those believers who, like me, believe that the local church is God's instrument to reach the world with His great news of the gospel. And it's written to motivate those leaders who long to see their labor yield much greater fruit for God's kingdom.

My prayer is that this book will have a part in moving thousands of churches toward greater ministry impact and help thousands of boards become high-impact boards.

T. J. Addington
Big Sky, Montana

HOW TO USE THIS BOOK

If you are a senior pastor or leadership-board member, do not read this book alone! All that will cause is frustration, because change happens only with shared understanding, honest interaction, and common commitments. The reason we have too few high-impact boards is that leaders are often not on the same page.

Church-leadership boards need to read this book together. And, if boards read it together, then key staff members need to read it as well, as the two groups are either "dancing" well together or are stepping on one another's toes. In addition, I would encourage you to use this book as part of your training for new board and staff members, to help ensure a common understanding of your leadership paradigm.

As you read together, engage in robust dialogue. You'll benefit if you adopt an attitude of "nothing to prove and nothing to lose." What worked at a prior stage in your church life may not work well now, so don't be afraid to acknowledge needed changes. Healthy boards do not protect the status quo if there is a better practice.

Do pay attention to the High-Impact Moments and Best Practices ("H. I. Moment" and "H. I. Best Practice") spread throughout the book. Consider and discuss the questions together. There will be junctures where the board will need to stop and ask, "What should we change here?" And then commit to putting that change into action. Your board will earn the title "high impact" because of how you operate, not how much you know.

Chapter One

THE HIGH-IMPACT REVOLUTION

Let's face it: For too long we have settled for too little in the local church. We have not embraced Christ's promise of "much fruit, copious fruit" (see John 15) but have been content with modest fruit. We have allowed our church structures to hinder and handicap ministry initiatives. We have allowed accidental ministry to characterize our leadership. And we have allowed our structures to creak along unchanged, decade after decade, making leadership a chore.

High-Impact Church Boards is written for leaders who want to see their churches become everything they can be under God—those who want to maximize the missional impact of their congregations. It is for those not content with the status quo, who believe a high-impact board is not only possible but is the only kind of leadership Christ would want for His church. It is for those who want healthier leaders and more intentional leadership paradigms, who long for empowered leadership structures and congregational cultures.

This is also a practical book. It is written primarily for leadership practitioners, not academicians. As a church leader, you want tools that work and tools that are biblical. So do I. While I avidly read both secular and religious leadership books and have learned much from them, the heart of this material comes out of my understanding of what God has called church leaders to be and do. It comes, as well, from having lived in the real world of church leadership for more than three decades.

Like you, I have seen the great, the good, the bad, and the ugly along the way. I want to help church leaders move to the great, never settle for the good, and deal effectively with the bad and the ugly. If I could make one promise to you through this book, it would be just that.

HIGH-IMPACT LEADERSHIP

Everything in this book focuses on what I call high-impact leadership. When I begin a consultation with a church, I usually ask key staff members and members of the senior board of a church (and leaders of other elected committees and boards) to identify the leadership issues that trouble them. As I record the concerns on a whiteboard, we all see the results. Almost without exception, the issues fall into one of three areas: the board and how it does leadership; the intentionality (or lack of it) in ministry; and the frustrations of getting stuff done and decisions made. *Where does mistrust of leaders fit?*

I am convinced that these three areas demand our attention. Multiplied together, they lead our boards toward what I call a high-impact revolution. The first factor in the equation is **healthy leaders**—the health of church leaders and clarity in what God has called them to do. This is the focus of the first section of the book.

The second factor is **intentional leadership**—a commitment to deeply intentional ministry rather than accidental ministry. The second section provides a simple, workable paradigm for moving your congregation in the direction God is calling you. *example: swing dancing*

The third factor is **empowered leadership structures**—friendly structures and an empowered church culture that allows leaders to lead and participants to minister. Too many churches have controlling and permission-withholding cultures rather than empowering and permission-granting cultures. This is the focus of the third section of the book.

Our problem is that it is not the leaders, or the structures, who are permission-withholding: it is the people, esp those who give.

· let them die off? · cut them off (disband Maranantha?) · call them o · sell the building?

Paying attention to these three areas will revolutionize the leadership impact of your board and the ministry impact of your congregation. Show me any high-impact congregation, and you will find that they got these three areas right.

WHAT'S YOUR ROM?

Those in the business world are familiar with the term ROI (return on investment). Successful business depends on the ROI. If the return on investment is not healthy, the business declines rather than grows.

I believe church boards need to pay great attention to another return: "return on mission," or "ROM." Christ has granted to you opportunity, resources, fruit, and a unique ministry to touch your community, your region, and the world. So, what is your ROM? My prayer is that, as you read these principles and practices, you will see an annual increase in your ROM. *What do we measure? How?*

High-impact boards do not happen by accident. They start with a conviction among leaders that we will not be satisfied until we lead our church in a way that maximizes ministry impact. To settle for anything less is unacceptable for the church of Christ.

H. I. MOMENT

When I engage in a leadership consultation with a church, I often ask, "What are your deliverables or outcomes?" and "Tell me about your organization's decision-making process." To help you answer those questions, respond to the following twenty questions by circling yes or no. Think about your church's leadership board and governance system as you answer.

1. Are you ever frustrated by the pace of decision-making? Yes (No)
2. Is it necessary to get approval from more than one group in order to get something done? Yes (No)
3. Do you ever find your board revisiting issues you thought were settled? (Yes) No
4. Is there confusion or conflict over the place the congregation, staff, or board plays in leadership or decision-making? (Yes) No   *Tho rarely among the Board.*
5. Does your board have a clear job description and understand its responsibilities? Yes (No)
6. Does the board spend more time managing day-to-day activities than thinking and planning for the future? Yes (No)
7. Can you identify the "preferred future" for your congregation, and is this a shared dream of the board? (Yes) No
8. Do your board and staff members work from clear annual ministry goals and plans? Yes (No)
9. Are you frustrated with the number of decisions that need to go to the congregation for approval? Yes (No)
10. Is there a high level of unity and relational health among board members? (Yes) No
11. Do your church structure and bylaws hinder rather than help leaders make timely decisions? Yes (No)
12. Does your board have ample time for prayer and study of Scripture and to dream and plan for the future? Yes (No)

· Current example: swing dancing

· Past example: Gloria concert

13. Does your board have a covenant that spells out its procedural and relational practices?   Yes (No)
14. Has the lack of such a covenant ever caused problems for the board? (Yes) No
15. Does the church have a process designed to find the very best leaders for your senior board? (Yes) No
16. Do you have a process to mentor and train potential leaders before they become leaders? (Yes) No
17. Do you believe your church is maximizing its ministry impact?   Yes (No)
18. Does your congregation have more than one elected board?   Yes (No)
19. Is there tension or confusion between the staff and board over who is responsible for what?   Yes (No)
20. Are you able to attract and retain the best leaders in your church to serve on your senior-leadership board?   Yes (No)

Scoring

How many yes answers do you have? _7_.
> A perfect score would be a yes for questions 5, 7, 8, 10, 12, 13, 15, 16, 17, 20.   10

How many no answers do you have? _13_.
> A perfect score would be a no for questions 1, 2, 3, 4, 6, 9, 11, 14, 18, 19.   10

Talk It Over

Find out how each member of your board answered these questions, and discuss the results together. The conversation will help you identify issues in your church-leadership paradigm that need to be changed if you are going to maximize your congregation's ministry impact.

If you take this book seriously and if you are willing to work through this book as a board (and as senior staff members), you can get to a perfect score above. You can become a high-impact board that leads with great intentionality within an empowered structure and culture.

Part One

HEALTHY LEADERS

If anyone sets his heart on being an overseer, he desires a noble task.

— 1 TIMOTHY 3:1

Chapter Two

THE HIGH CALLING OF LEADERSHIP

Leadership is an awe-inspiring, weighty calling. From the earliest days of biblical history, God has called men and women into leadership roles, energizing and gifting them for the task. One lesson shouts from the pages in this history of God's people: *When there was a faithful leader, God's people flourished. In the absence of godly, empowered leadership, His people suffered.*

Without a Noah, mankind would not have survived. Without a Moses, the Exodus would have failed. Without a Joshua, the land would not have been conquered. Without a Deborah, the Israelites would not have been liberated. Without a David, a nation would not have been built. Without a Nehemiah, a city would not have been reborn. Without an Esther, a people would not have survived.

In each instance, God called a leader or leaders for His purposes, clarified their assignments, and empowered them with skill and wisdom. In God's kingdom, leaders are called by Him for His purposes and empowered by His Spirit. We do not just choose to be a leader; God chooses those He wants to lead.

CALLING CHANGES EVERYTHING

It is now more than thirty years since I first served in some capacity of congregational leadership. At times it has been exhilarating. At other times, deeply painful. Church leadership is not for the faint of heart, the easily discouraged, the impatient, or those who live for quick results. In a church full of volunteers, leaders can't just fire someone who's screwing

How about me?

21

Neither can a corp.

up or making life difficult. We have to work with whoever comes, and those who come are — like us — sinners: imperfect, unique, from differing backgrounds, and carrying plenty of personal baggage.

Then the dimension of spiritual warfare is added to this. Our battle, Paul said, is not against flesh and blood but against the spiritual forces of the universe (see Ephesians 6:12). In this spiritually broken world, God has chosen communities of Christ followers as His divine means to bring grace and healing to people estranged from Him. His opponent, Satan, is fiercely engaged in trying to obstruct God's grace from flowing into broken lives. The spiritual battle rages with its greatest intensity right where we lead — in the church.

At a number of junctures along the way in my leadership roles — usually when a congregation had been experiencing pain and leaders had to make difficult decisions — I've been asked, "Why do you stay in leadership?" That's a great question. My answer is that I have been called to lead. Calling makes all the difference! This is the way I can serve the most important institution on earth. I am not just doing my time; I am fulfilling God's call on my life.   *Me?*

Peter underscored the divine nature of this calling in his words to leaders in 1 Peter 5:

> To the elders among you, I appeal as a fellow elder, a witness
> of Christ's sufferings and one who also will share in the glory
> to be revealed: Be shepherds of God's flock that is under your
> care, serving as overseers — not because you must, but because
> you are willing, as God wants you to be; not greedy for money,
> but eager to serve; not lording it over those entrusted to you, but
> being examples to the flock. (verses 1-3)

The call to leadership brings an eternal reward. Peter reminded us of the eternal value God places on church leadership by concluding with a promise for those who serve well: "And when the Chief Shepherd appears, you will receive the crown of glory that will never fade away" (verse 4).

Church leadership is a sacred task given by the Lord to a few to ensure the health of His people and the expansion of His kingdom. A called leader is an effective leader, one characterized by godly influence, by action, and by giftedness.

CALLED TO INFLUENCE

When my sons were young, I worked as the executive director of ministry advancement for the Evangelical Free Church of America (EFCA). My boys had a simplistic notion of what it was like to be a "boss" (their word). In their view, every problem I faced at work could be easily solved. After all, I had the power to tell people what to do and they did it (wow!), to hire and fire at will (anyone hear of *due process?*), and to spend money wherever I desired (what, budgets?). In their innocent eyes, leadership was a blast—and easy. It was certainly efficient.

I am sure there *are* some organizations like that and equally sure that, apart from the leader, no one wants to work there. This kind of "positional" leadership fits neither the church nor the leadership style Christ taught His disciples. In the church, leaders gain and influence followers by the integrity of their lives, the consistency between their words and actions, their demonstrated commitment to follow Christ, and their humility and service.

In the passage from 1 Peter, Peter told elders, "Be shepherds of God's flock that is under your care, serving as overseers," and then gave three qualifiers of healthy leadership.

1. *"Not because you must, but because you are willing."* Good leaders do not lead out of obligation. They lead because they are willing to answer Christ's call with happy hearts, knowing it is a privilege to serve as leaders. Obligation creates frustration when things don't go our way. Willing hearts create generous leaders who freely give of their time, energy, and leadership skills, knowing they do so on behalf of Jesus.

Status prestige

2. *"Not greedy for money, but eager to serve."* The second quality of healthy leaders is that they are not in it for selfish reasons. Their motivation does not come out of self-interest — whether a paycheck for full-time leaders or recognition for lay leaders. Instead, they are motivated to express leadership through serving those they lead.

3. *"Not lording it over those entrusted to you, but being examples to the flock."* Healthy leaders do not lead out of position and power but out of their very lives. The true test of a leader is whether anyone is following. I might grudgingly acquiesce to a supervisor when I feel coerced, because that is what I must do to keep my job. But I will only *follow* those I trust and respect and whose lives validate their worthiness to be followed.

Peter said leadership is not about power and positional authority (like my kids once thought) but about setting the pace in character, ministry, service, and spiritual growth. *Great leadership is influence* that comes from selfless passion to serve. So how is leadership different from disciple-making?

After a number of years where Americans have tried to disengage character from leadership, we are again learning the biblical lesson that character counts. The June 7, 2002, Money section of *USA Today* featured a former CEO accused of trying to evade $1 million in taxes on artwork he had purchased — after receiving $19 million in cash and some $80 million in stock over recent years. Coming on the heels of the Arthur Andersen and Enron accounting scandals, investors were jumping ship in droves from this CEO's company. In just one day, the company's shares fell dramatically, wiping out $5.4 billion in market value.

Does character count? Evidently those stockholders thought so. Ironically, this man had recently given a high school graduation speech in New Hampshire, where he told the students, "You will be confronted with questions every day that test your morals. . . . Think carefully, and for your sake, do the right thing, not the easy thing."

We know from experience how quickly the influence of church

THE HIGH CALLING OF LEADERSHIP

leaders vanishes when they are found to be living double lives. Why is this? Quite simply, the integrity of our lives is inseparably linked with our influence. High integrity brings with it a high degree of influence and, therefore, leadership capital. When integrity is lacking, influence decreases and leadership capital is lost (and not easily restored).

So why have we lost leadership capital?

The apostle Paul felt so strongly about the connection between character and leadership that in both 1 Timothy and Titus he listed qualifications for those who desire to lead in the church. These character qualities include how well leaders manage their own emotions and lives, the quality of leadership within their homes, and their spiritual maturity and reputation in the marketplace. In other words, character counts in all areas of life.

It is not enough to understand strategy and direction. The world is full of leaders who grasp tactics and execution but whose careless character leaves them with little influence among those they desire to lead. Thus, the call to lead is also a call to authentic, transparent living in which the leader walks the walk and talks the talk.

Do I walk the talk?

BIASED TOWARD ACTION

Another quality of those Christ has called to lead His flock on His behalf is that they are active rather than passive. Many church boards need to confront the reality that they have been acting as passive trustees rather than proactive leaders. When this happens, they miss the role they have been called to play and the mission Christ left for the church.

Consider Christ's instructions to His followers: "Therefore go and make disciples of all nations, baptizing them in the name of the Father and of the Son and of the Holy Spirit, and teaching them to obey everything I have commanded you. And surely I am with you always, to the very end of the age" (Matthew 28:19-20).

There is nothing passive in this mission! We are to aggressively take territory for Jesus in our cities, our nation, and our world. This is a picture of Christ followers on the move, bringing real change to communities, institutions, marketplaces, and families. One mark of a successful ministry is the presence of leaders with an extraordinary bias toward action.

What does this mean for those of us who are not naturally strong leaders? The books of 1 and 2 Timothy fascinate me because they are the counsel to Timothy from Paul, a strong, action-biased mentor. It seems that Timothy was a rather shy, conflict-avoiding, reluctant leader. Paul, on the other hand, was a natural-born leader. I am intrigued by Paul's advice to Timothy, because, like him, most of us don't fit the natural-born leader profile, to whom active leadership comes innately.

As we read the letters from Paul to Timothy, we hear Paul giving instructions on basic leadership principles: resolving conflict, training leaders, teaching boldly, correcting error, leading by example, living authentically, refusing to be intimidated by bullies—and any number of practical skills. Because Paul believed Christ had called Timothy and that Timothy was willing to learn and grow, he encouraged Timothy in his leadership role.

Likewise, those who have been called to pastoral or board roles must by necessity become students of leadership. If we believe that leadership in the church is a sacred task given to a few by Christ to ensure the health of His people and the expansion of His kingdom, we must be willing to grow in our understanding of what effective leadership looks like and learn to become better leaders.

In addition to godly influence and a bias toward action, a called leader will also be divinely gifted by God for the role.

GIFTED AND WIRED TO LEAD

Knowing potential leaders' gifts and wiring is crucial for effective leadership. In the marketplace, huge energy and money are expended to get the right people into the right spot based on abilities and wiring. In the church, far too little attention is paid to this, even though the New Testament clearly articulates the principle.

Perhaps one of the reasons so many churches in the United States are at a plateau or in decline is that we have not asked enough *leaders*

Many sheep say " If leadership does something that hurts or confuse me, then it is wrong, and they are untrustworthy leaders."

to lead and have paid little attention to where we deploy individuals in relation to their God-given gift sets. My experience is that nominating committees (or whoever serves as the gatekeepers asking others to serve) are recruiting people into key ministry roles, though they have received little or no training regarding giftedness.

Christ has given each believer a set of gifts. When properly deployed, believers are in their "sweet spot"—where they can make the best contribution to His kingdom, with joy. One spiritual gift is leadership (see Romans 12:8). Another closely tied to it is administration (see 1 Corinthians 12:28). Certainly, those we ask to serve in leadership roles should have leadership or administrative gifts *among* their abilities even if it's not their primary gift.

H. I. BEST PRACTICE

Always consider wiring and gifting in choosing individuals for any leadership or ministry position.

Wisdom (and Scripture) suggests we ought to task individuals according to their gifts and their unique wiring, not according to openings we might have. Too often, however, we do the latter to satisfy our organizational structure. The result is unfair frustration for individuals, ineffectiveness in their roles, and a *net loss* for the congregation. I have met board members who are frustrated because they are gifted in areas other than leadership, so their leadership role makes them uncomfortable and ineffective. If you are reading this and are outside your area of giftedness and place of joyful ministry, you know exactly what I mean. It is even possible that after reading this book you may conclude God has not called you to a leadership role.

Does this mean that only individuals who have a *primary* giftedness of leadership should be asked to serve on the leadership board of a church? I would answer "not necessarily"—with several qualifications. First, Christ has given the gift of leadership, and those with the gift should be deployed accordingly. Second, many have leadership or administration *within* their gift mix. While these gifts may not be primary, these people can lead effectively. Third—and this is the crucial point—*all who agree to serve in leadership must be willing to grow in their leadership skills and to fulfill the various dimensions of leadership even when it is difficult.*   Is this me?

I am also convinced that we ought to pay closer attention to the difference between leadership and caring gifts. The *primary* gifts needed to lead are fundamentally different from those needed to fulfill a caring function. People in crisis need caregivers who are high on mercy, under-standing, and patience. Those with strong leadership gifts are often not great at "feeling your pain." Similarly, high-mercy individuals often find conflict difficult, and leadership brings its share (good and bad); lead-ers must make many decisions that are going to cause unhappiness for some person or group. I have encountered high-mercy types in senior-leadership roles who feel totally out of their comfort zone. They serve because they were asked, but the experience is painful and frustrating.

Identifying called leaders according to their gifting doesn't mean that everyone will lead in the same way. Leaders have a specific profile that makes them effective, even as they lead through a variety of styles. For example, pastors are leaders by definition. Yet many pastors do not consider leadership as one of their primary gifts. Part of the reason for this self-evaluation is that many pastors unfairly compare themselves with high-profile, natural-born leaders. But there are a variety of leader-ship styles, and even those who are naturally introverted can lead well. More profound than our assessments is the truth that those Christ calls to leadership—pastoral or volunteer—can grow (and should be grow-ing) in their leadership skills. Good leadership is more learned than innate.

Strong, high-impact leadership boards are made up of individuals who have leadership or administrative gifts within their gift sets, are action-oriented, are people of proven influence, and are willing to carry out all the New Testament–given functions of senior church leaders.

THE PROFILE OF AN EFFECTIVE, CALLED CHURCH LEADER

If we desire high-impact boards, we need to ask: "What are the characteristics of an effective, called church leader?" Before looking at the answer, consider some of the ways churches traditionally fill leadership roles:

Inclusion criteria

exclusion criteria

- We look for godly individuals.
- We give the nod to those who have "power" in the church.
- We try to balance "power blocks" in the church by making sure each block is represented on the board.
- We use an unofficial system that rotates key people through the leadership spots.
- We choose people who have been in the church a long time.
- Congregations simply nominate people; if nominees have the votes, they end up on the board regardless of gifting or qualifications.
- We fill leadership slots even when there is a lack of qualified candidates.

Clearly, none of these methods will result in a board with great effectiveness or impact. Nor are these methods likely to motivate those with true leadership gifts to serve.

The way we choose leaders and our understanding of what good leadership looks like go to the heart of church health and ministry impact. In this chapter, we've already looked at some of these characteristics. Now let's examine an expanded list of the marks of an effective leader, whether for senior staff teams or leadership boards. As we consider a leader's calling, we should begin to see these elements in his or her profile.

① Exhibits godly character and lifestyle. This is the most critical, nonnegotiable characteristic of a church leader. We are called to lead on behalf of Jesus Christ, as shepherds accountable to the Chief Shepherd (see 1 Peter 5:4). Paul made it clear in 1 Timothy and Titus that, above all else, a leader's life must be in the process of being transformed into the likeness of Christ. Only those deeply committed to personal transformation and authenticity can lead others in that direction.

It has often been said that money, sex, and power are the universal tests of character—good and bad. The New Testament addresses all of these as it discusses leadership. God's leaders are not to be obsessed with money or greed (see 1 Timothy 3:3); they are to be people of sexual fidelity and purity (see 1 Timothy 3:2); and they are to be committed to serve people rather than desiring power (see 1 Peter 5:2-3). Questionable character has *no place* in church leadership. On the positive side, authentic godly character stands out and says something powerful about the church and the Lord we represent.

(2) **Influences others positively.** As we saw earlier, real leaders influence others whether or not they are in positions of leadership. And that influence must be *positive*. Bullies have influence (and yes, there are a few in the church), but it is not life-giving.

When considering people for leadership roles, ask the following key questions: "Do they already have a positive influence over others? Do people look to them for leadership? Do they lead people closer to Christ and in positive ministry directions?" *Am I an influencer?*

(3) **Exhibits a bias toward action.** We also considered that leaders *do* things! They have a bias away from the status quo and toward action. They don't always know *what* to do, but they will try things and see what works. Leaders are never content with how things are but dream of how they could be, continually looking for ways to accomplish mission more effectively.

The natural tendency of groups is to settle into a comfort zone. Yet the mission Christ left the church is a proactive one that requires the best thinking, best practices, best strategy, best execution, and a continual push by leaders toward the active involvement of all of God's people. Leaders regularly stir things up and attempt to move people out of comfort zones into active involvement on behalf of Christ and His kingdom.

but our people want that! How can we help them want something better?

④ **Holds a deep passion for Jesus.** The church is about Jesus! He is its leader, and leaders serve under Him. Thus, only those with a passion for Jesus are qualified to lead His people. It is painfully obvious when church leaders are more interested in their own agendas than in leading Christ's people where He wants them to go. If living in intimacy with Christ and leading others into intimacy with Him is not the leader's deepest concern, he or she will lead His people to places He does not want them to go.

A sobering truth is that few congregations rise above the spiritual level of their leaders. The higher their passion for Jesus, the higher their congregation's passion will be. In the end, without a passion for Christ, they have missed the whole point of the Christian life and their leadership roles.

⑤ **Displays personal humility.** Leadership in the church differs in two significant respects from how it is often practiced in other arenas. First, it is a leadership of service rather than power. As Peter wrote, overseers should be "eager to serve; not lording it over those entrusted to you" (1 Peter 5:2-3). Second, this leadership already has its agenda set by the Lord of the church. The leadership priorities are Christ's, not our own. The character trait of humility is crucial for leaders who must submit their will to the Head of the church, work in a team setting, and lead by godly example.

I have seen ego-driven individuals hungry for power and influence elbow their way into church leadership. Once in control, they have little concern for the spiritual health of the congregation. Positions of spiritual leadership are ego aphrodisiacs for some, and it is not pleasant to be around such folks when they don't get their way.

⑥ **Loves people genuinely.** The driving characteristic of God's pursuit of us is an unexplainable, powerful, unrelenting love bathed in mercy, compassion, forgiveness, and grace. The apostle John said that the defining mark of a Christ follower is love (see 1 John 3:11-24). Ego-driven individuals love themselves, not others. Humble, godly individuals love others as Christ loves, and their leadership is fueled by genuine spiritual concern.

⑦ **Learns throughout life.** Nowhere is it more important for leaders to be lifelong learners than in the context of the local church. There are three areas where church leaders ought to give high priority to ongoing learning.

One is Scripture. Too many church leaders settle for a superficial level of biblical knowledge. Yet our ability to lead our congregations into the depths of life and ministry is directly dependent on the thoroughness of our understanding of God's Word.

We must also be students of effective ministry methods. What worked in the past may not work today. We continually need to explore effective ways to communicate the gospel, connect people, and help them grow and become engaged in ministry in ways that are effective in our day and culture.

Healthy leaders are also students of leadership. Leadership in the church continues to become more complex, with the heightened differences between worldviews and cultures, with the increasingly secular nature of those coming into our churches, and with the challenges of keeping congregations healthy. Once leaders give up learning as a high value, their effective leadership days are over.

⑧ **Focuses on the team.** Leadership teams require *team* players. Those who cannot function as a healthy member of a team will destroy the unity necessary for a leadership board to function. Never elect or appoint to leadership an individual who cannot work graciously in a team setting—and publicly and privately support decisions the team has made.

Mature, healthy leaders choose to subordinate their egos to the will of the group (remember the characteristic "displays personal humility"). They are committed to supporting group decisions unless they cannot affirm them in good conscience because of a clear moral issue. Mature leaders *never* undermine decisions of the board or force decisions by underhanded means. They are, as one of Paul's requirements for leadership states, "not quarrelsome" (1 Timothy 3:3). Healthy leaders also recognize that God has not gifted us all alike, nor do any of us have all wisdom. Healthy leaders deeply value the perspectives and input of

- Giving advice
- Taking orders

others and the collective decisions of the board.

If any board member is unwilling to operate in the context of a team, the board must be willing to confront lovingly and, if necessary, remove that individual from the board. Many boards and congregations have suffered conflict and division from "lone rangers" (well-intentioned or not) who cared more about their agendas than about the health of the leadership team or the church.

(9) **Leads willingly.** Good leaders are willing leaders, as we saw in 1 Peter 5. Willing leaders are ready to make sacrifices without inner resentment and frustration. *Me?*

It is a mistake to coerce individuals to serve in leadership positions. When we push people to serve before they are mature enough to handle the difficulties of leadership (such as conflict), they often have experiences that cause them to avoid future leadership. When a young leader (either in faith or chronological years) says, "I am not ready," wisdom dictates that we take that response seriously and continue to mentor that person toward leadership in the future.

(10) **Extends hope.** Leaders are optimistic about the future and convey that optimism and hope to those they lead. They believe that positive things can and will happen because they understand it is God who empowers and it is He who has promised to be with the church until the end of the age.

Pessimists are not leaders! Pessimists telegraph caution and see all the reasons something cannot happen. Healthy leaders are like Nehemiah, who in the hopelessness around him conveyed an exciting future based on his trust in a sovereign God. Whatever you think of their politics, this was the genius of leaders such as Franklin Roosevelt, Ronald Reagan, and one of my all-time heroes, Winston Churchill. Like Nehemiah, they were purveyors of contagious hope.

(11) **Understands and agrees with God's leadership assignment.** I often ask leadership boards if they can clearly articulate their responsibilities. Invariably, apart from generalities, the answer is no. I believe God has given leaders a defined set of responsibilities, which I call Six-Dimensional Leadership (we will explore this in the next two chapters). I encourage

every leadership board to define its set of responsibilities as part of studying this book.

⑫ **Grapples with the future.** To lead is to be out in front. True leadership is primarily about the future and secondarily about the present. While this may seem obvious, most leadership boards spend the majority of their time on present issues. *Or are haunted by the past.*

One can lead by managing crisis, managing the status quo, or managing the future. While leaders must manage crisis from time to time, the very definition of a leader—someone out front, helping to move people where they need to go—requires management of the future. This means leaders need to be willing to give up details of many present-day issues to qualified people so they can spend time thinking, learning, praying, and guiding their congregations into a rich future. (When we examine the six dimensions of church leadership, you'll notice that each dimension requires a future focus and a bias toward action.)

⑬ **Leads boldly.** Many church leaders face a significant fear factor that prevents bold leadership. What if our decisions make people unhappy? Some probably will; leadership always gets pushback of some kind.

Unfortunately, boards have not learned to lead boldly, leaving the church one of the most leaderless institutions in America. We have more fear than courage. You may take issue with me. However, think about it: Why it is that despite the number of churches, the gospel is making so little impact on our communities? Satan must rejoice over this general condition. Timid leaders don't threaten him. Bold and healthy leaders keep him highly occupied.

Almost without exception, congregations that are truly making a difference in their communities and experiencing real life change within their bodies are led by a godly, healthy, bold, energized leadership team—pastoral and volunteer.

CALLING BOLD LEADERS

Because many boards have not grappled with critical leadership issues, they live with a high degree of frustration. But there is hope! Over the past decade, I have watched many frustrated boards become energized, active, and even high impact as they have made the choice to lead with greater boldness. This can be true for your board as well, as you learn to choose leaders who have been called by God into this role and who exhibit the qualities of called, effective church leaders. Once we understand the concept of being *called* into leadership, it changes our perspectives when faced with difficult issues and people. If Christ has called us to leadership, we can lead with boldness.

Many of us do not have training in leadership. This is often true of pastors; even though much of a pastor's ministry relates to leadership, few have received leadership training or mentoring (and seminaries aren't stepping up to the plate fast enough). The good news for all of us is: We can learn to lead! There are few natural-born leaders. Most of us are "leaders in training" and will always be learning to lead more effectively. As Paul said, if we are going to lead, we must "govern diligently" (Romans 12:8).

As one with leadership gifts, I can think of no more exciting arena in which to use them than the church of Jesus Christ. Amazingly, notwithstanding the challenges, difficulties, and problems, Christ has chosen the local church as His means to reach the world with His good news. He has never given up on the church, and neither can we. Our challenge is to grow in our ability to lead well so that leadership is a joy rather than a burden, and to lead in ways that allow Christ to fulfill our congregations' mission in the expansion of His kingdom.

Leadership matters. It matters to God because the quality of our leadership has direct impact on the depth of His disciples and the effectiveness of His mission. Lead boldly!

H. I. MOMENT

Does our board have a profile of what an effective and healthy leader looks like — something we've conveyed to those who choose leaders in our church?

How does gifting fit into our leadership profile?

We have picked on character service, not leadership.

Are we intentional in choosing leaders? Do any of the traditional ways congregations choose church leaders apply to us? Do we need to consider modifications in our selection procedure? *— our role — prime the pump*

Is our board's leadership passive, modest, or bold? Is it a healthy or unhealthy model? Why?

Take three minutes to complete the following sentence and share your thoughts with one another: "Based on this chapter I believe we need to _____."

reject the past!

H. I. WRAP-UP: PROFILE OF AN EFFECTIVE CHURCH LEADER

- Exhibits godly character and lifestyle
- Influences others positively
- Exhibits a bias toward action
- Holds a deep passion for Jesus
- Displays personal humility
- Loves people genuinely
- Learns throughout life
- Focuses on the team
- Leads willingly
- Extends hope
- Understands and agrees with God's leadership assignment
- Grapples with the future
- Leads boldly

How to distinguish harsh and sharp from bold?

Chapter Three

SIX-DIMENSIONAL LEADERSHIP, PART ONE

Thailand is one of my all-time favorite places. In the north, cities such as Chiang Mai and Chiang Rai straddle the ancient and the modern. In the south lie some of the world's most pristine beaches. And then there is the capital, Bangkok, which you'll either love or hate. Depending on your mood, it is either a bustling, fascinating, beautiful, and ever-changing city, or a dark, polluted, hot, crowded metropolis. Usually it is both at once.

Splitting the metropolis in two is the Chao Phraya River. No visit to Bangkok is complete without a ride on the longboat water taxis that ply the river and the narrow canals entering and exiting it.

I was riding one of these water taxis when I first noticed a beautiful hotel whose brilliant-blue glass face reaches some thirty stories high. After seeing it on several visits to Bangkok, I became increasingly curious. By day, it looks like any number of the gracious five-star hotels lining the meandering river. It isn't until the sun fades that this luxury hotel appears different from the others. Then, unlike the other brilliantly lit hotels, no lights appear in any of the soaring windows.

Upon some detective work, I discovered this building is empty. After its initial construction, authorities discovered the magnificent structure had a fatal, foundational flaw that caused it to tilt to one side. The hotel will never be occupied, and once litigation is complete, it will be demolished. Each time I see it, I marvel at the extreme cost of an engineering mistake that started with the very foundation.

In the previous chapter, I mentioned we would address six dimensions of high-impact church leaders; I call this Six-Dimensional Leadership. In this chapter, we will examine the most foundational of these leadership responsibilities (the next chapter will explore the rest of the dimensions). When I teach church boards about these God-given responsibilities, we talk about:

1. Ensuring spiritual power
2. Teaching
3. Protecting
4. Caring
5. Developing, empowering, and releasing
6. Leading

For me, that Bangkok hotel illustrates the first—and key—dimension. The building—beautiful on the outside, foundationally flawed, and empty of guests—is a metaphor for many ministries today. These ministries appear successful in numbers, facilities, strategies, and staffing but are fatally flawed in their very foundations: They lack the power of the God they are designed to serve.

LEADERSHIP DIMENSION ONE: ENSURING SPIRITUAL POWER

"Apart from me you can do nothing," Jesus proclaimed in John 15:5. These seven words ought to strike fear in the heart of every church leader. In John 15—a key passage for all who would lead—Jesus taught the necessity of an organic connection between Himself and His followers. Consider these words in the context of your church and personal life:

No branch can bear fruit by itself; it must remain in the vine. Neither can you bear fruit unless you remain in me. I am the vine; you are the branches. If a man [or ministry] remains in me and I in him, he will bear much fruit; apart from me you can do nothing. (verses 4-5)

Do you believe that? Nada—nothing—without Jesus? Before you answer, I'll confess I haven't always believed it. Not that I don't believe *Jesus*. But I have fooled myself numerous times into thinking I was capable of using my gifts and abilities to do significant things for Jesus without taking seriously the necessity of His power in my ministry endeavors. One of the reasons I could fool myself is that I *did* see results, and at times they looked pretty impressive. So my hand is raised; I have not always believed that apart from Him I can do nothing.

Many congregations don't believe it either. And we *can* manage many impressive accomplishments without much help from God. We can craft state-of-the-art worship services, teach excellent theology, design wonderful programs, build people-friendly buildings, see our congregations grow, send missionaries abroad, help the poor and forgotten, and accomplish any number of successful, impressive enterprises—without God's help. All it takes is some leadership, money, and volunteers, along with a bit of strategy and energy. And the more we pull it off, the more we don't believe these seven words of Jesus.

From the outside, what we build looks pretty good. But like the luxury hotel on the Chao Phraya River, something foundational is missing: The power isn't turned on. The building is empty.

EMPOWERED TO BEAR FRUIT

The issue is not whether we can accomplish the impressive but whether our energies will result in lasting results. We measure results in many ways: congregational size, percentage who attend small groups, Sunday-school turnout, budgets, programs, buildings, and staff members. Yet Jesus also has a measurement system for the church: spiritual fruit. "This is to my Father's glory, that you bear much fruit, showing yourselves to be my disciples. . . . I . . . appointed you to go and bear fruit—fruit that will last" (John 15:8,16).

In Jesus' kingdom and in His church, what matters is spiritual fruit—not merely results, as we often define them. Any group of leaders can get results without Jesus, but we cannot generate eternal, abundant

How to measure?

spiritual fruit ≠ spiritual "results"

fruit without His empowerment. What is the New Testament evidence of spiritual fruit?

- People coming into a personal relationship with God (see Mark 4:1-20; Luke 19:10; Philemon 6)
- A desire that Christ would change us into His likeness so we take on His character and priorities over time (see Colossians 3:1-17; 2 Peter 1:3-11)
- Becoming passionate about knowing Him through His Word and through intimacy with Him in prayer (see John 15; James 1:19-25)
- Obeying and following Christ in all parts of life as our highest priority (see 1 John 2:3-6)
- A love for others that grows and flourishes in our hearts, resulting in acts of kindness (see John 15:9-17)
- Obedience to Christ that causes us to engage in changing and influencing the world around us for Him (see 1 Peter 2:9-12)
- Becoming people who long to see eternal fruit come from our lives (see John 15:5,16; Colossians 1:10)
- Regular growth in the display of the Spirit's fruit in us (see Galatians 5:22-25)

In light of the call to bear *spiritual* fruit, some will be tempted to think that results don't matter. Actually, nothing could be further from the truth. Results do matter to God. The Great Commission sends us out into the world to make disciples—to bring people to Christ and to help them grow. Paul constantly enjoined us to get rid of the old nature and take on the new nature. Jesus wants to see more believers and better believers! But how do we bear this fruit? Jesus' picture in John 15 of the vine and the branches provides the answer.

More and better believers!

SPIRITUAL FRUIT COMES FROM REMAINING

Every day in ancient Palestine, Jesus' disciples walked past vineyards. They glimpsed decades-old gnarled vines with branches extending from them. Twice a year they observed farmers pruning back branches so they would yield more fruit. They knew that the better tended the vine, the better the fruit. So the vineyard was a familiar concept when Jesus used it as a metaphor to impress on His disciples the importance of an ongoing, intimate, and organic connection with Him. He wanted them to grasp that they would need this connection if they were going to experience lasting fruit in their lives and ministries.

> I am the true vine, and my Father is the gardener. He cuts off every branch in me that bears no fruit, while every branch that does bear fruit he prunes so that it will be even more fruitful. You are already clean because of the word I have spoken to you. *Remain* in me, and I will *remain* in you. No branch can bear fruit by itself; it must *remain* in the vine. Neither can you bear fruit unless you *remain* in me.
>
> I am the vine; you are the branches. If a man *remains* in me and I in him, he will bear much fruit; apart from me you can do nothing. If anyone does not *remain* in me, he is like a branch that is thrown away and withers; such branches are picked up, thrown into the fire and burned. If you *remain* in me and my words *remain* in you, ask whatever you wish, and it will be given you. This is to my Father's glory, that you bear much fruit, showing yourselves to be my disciples. (John 15:1-8, emphasis added)

Jesus started by making a crucial distinction: He is the vine, the source of our life and power; we are the branches, and we derive our life power from Him. This is why we cannot yield spiritual fruit by ourselves. No branch can bear fruit if it is not connected to the life-giving sap from the grapevine.

The critical word is *remain*, which Jesus used eight times in these eight verses. The picture is of sap flowing into the branches in a moment-by-moment relationship where the very life of the branch is dependent on its connection to the vine. Jesus knew well that our pride, our

God-given gifts, the stresses of life, and our forgetfulness will tempt us to pull away from this organic relationship. So He reminded us eight times how important it is that we *remain* intimately connected.

This connection is critical for leaders. Before we are called to lead, we are called to connect with Christ on a 24/7 basis. We must tend that connection as carefully as a vineyard owner tends his vines because our spiritual lives affect the whole congregation. In fact, the congregation will take its cues from leadership and will rarely rise collectively above the spiritual level of its leaders. Leaders who are committed to intimate connection with Jesus will build into their lives a set of practices that keeps them connected, including time with God, connection to God's Word, and talking with God in prayer.

Unhurried time with God is essential. One of the great love killers of our day—whether with our spouses, friends, family, or Jesus—is busyness. Yet intimacy takes time. "Unhurried time" is a daily space we establish to be with God with no distractions. For most of us, this will not happen without ruthless resolve.

In a well-tended vineyard, great care is taken to ensure that the branches are kept out of the dirt. If allowed to fall on the ground, they can rot, spoiling the grapes. Daily unhurried time is the way we keep ourselves out of the dirt and well connected to the source of life: Jesus, the true vine. When we neglect our connections, we hit the "dirt," our intimacy with Jesus suffers, and the fruit spoils.

We must discover and rediscover His Word. The quality of our connection to the vine has a direct correlation with our connection to the Word. This is true for every believer, but it is especially true for those of us who lead in the church. We cannot lead others where we have not gone. Our spiritual lives flourish and are fed by His Word.

I have a small number of heroes. One is a close friend I've known most of my life. He has built a hugely successful business across the Midwest, becoming a leader in his industry. He is also one of the wisest church leaders I know. What I love about him, though, is that even with all his success, his highest priority is to please God and know Jesus—and it shows. I can ask at any time what God is teaching him and receive an intriguing, insightful answer. He's one of those people from whom you learn something in each conversation. One of my friend's habits is to read through the Bible every year, discovering and rediscovering the depths of our God, His plan for our lives, and His instructions for the church. To keep the reading fresh, he will often choose a translation he has not read before. This reading fuels and fulfills his passion to know God.

Decisions we make for the church have a direct bearing on the spiritual lives of those we lead. Unless we make them out of a living connection with Jesus, nurtured by His living Word in our lives, we are like dead branches trying to help other branches bear fruit. It doesn't work.

Another practice that is essential to the leadership dimension of ensuring spiritual power is regular connection through prayer.

EMPOWERED THROUGH THE MINISTRY OF PRAYER

Leading with the power on will happen as we walk through each day talking to God in humble dependence, expecting Him to hear and answer. Prayerlessness leads to rotting branches in the dust. Prayerfulness leads to healthy branches that bear copious fruit. There are few commands repeated more often in Scripture than the command, and encouragement, to pray.

There are some essential truths to keep in mind as we develop this connection with the vine.

Prayerful, expectant dependence is a hallmark of leaders. Men and women who are intimately connected to Jesus pray — a lot. They pray for spiritual results in their lives, and they pray with great expectancy that God will actually *answer* their prayers. Consider again John 15, where Jesus made a series of breathtaking promises:

- If we remain in Christ, we *will* bear fruit (verse 5).
- If we remain in Christ, we may ask *whatever we wish* related to fruit (in the context of these verses) and God will grant it (verse 7).

- God will answer our prayers because it is to the Father's glory that we bear *abundant fruit*, showing ourselves to be Christ's disciples (verse 8).

Christ's promise here is unequivocal: Those who remain in Him—and ask—will bear fruit. If we are not seeing fruit, we are either not *remaining* (staying intimately connected with Jesus) or we are not *asking.* Jesus repeated this promise in John 15:16: "You did not choose me, but I chose you and appointed you to go and bear fruit—fruit that will last. Then the Father will give you whatever you ask in my name." As His children, we were chosen by Christ and *appointed* (specifically commissioned) to bear eternal fruit.

Prayer is hard work. It is much easier to write and talk about prayer than to pray—especially for action-oriented leaders, for whom it is often more satisfying to "get something done" than to be still and pray. Most married couples find it a challenge to schedule quality time where they actually share their innermost hearts. How much harder to schedule time with someone we don't see, to quiet our minds (which often seems to invite them to roam to other issues), and to communicate with someone who doesn't usually speak audibly.

Intimacy, though, requires time with our Lover—unhurried time—and the expression of our hearts and souls. When we pray, we enter into God's presence in the most intimate way we will ever do this side of heaven. Though it may not always feel like it, in prayer we commune with a personal God who longs for us to know Him and bear abundant fruit for Him. We cannot remain in His presence without being changed; the more time we spend with Him, the more our lives begin to take on His character.

Though prayer that brings us into God's presence is hard work, it also lessens our effort as it releases God's work and power on our behalf. The book of James echoes Jesus' promises in John 15: "You do not have, because you do not ask God" (4:2). In my younger days, I often exerted a lot of energy on God's behalf with too little thought given to prayer. Today, I realize that if I spend more time with God, He paves the way for ministry success in His supernatural way, multiplying my effectiveness.

Active listening is essential. Does God speak to us? Do you believe God wants to talk to you on a regular basis? The picture of the vine and the branches shouts its answer: Yes! This is, after all, a picture of the vine's sap flowing into the branches 24/7.

The question is not, "Does God speak?" The question is, "Do we hear?" God rarely shouts. He comes in a gentle whisper to our souls. Unless we learn to hear, that gentle whisper is often drowned out by the din of life.

In my work I have experienced His gentle whisper numerous times. I don't have the wisdom or the answers to deal with all the issues that pop up. Many times, not knowing the direction to follow, I have committed these situations to prayer, mulled them over, and waited. Then, on my drive into work or in the course of my day, an answer comes like a light-bulb going on and I know what to do. My brilliance? No, God's gentle whisper of divine guidance just when I need it. Sometimes the answer is so good that I think, *I could never have figured that out.* That's true — I didn't; God did.

How can we learn to hear His gentle whisper? We start by telling God we desire to hear His voice more clearly. My own life changed when I said, "Lord, I believe You want to talk to me more often than I hear You. Would You help me hear more clearly and sensitize me to when You are trying to whisper to me? Help me distinguish between my thoughts and Your nudges to my soul."

H. I. MOMENT

Take a few minutes and jot down what are you hearing from God for the following areas:

- My life _____
- My work_____
- My leadership_*trust boldly*_____
- My church_*lead confidently*_____
- My family_____

If you are not hearing anything currently, try using the prayer above and then practice paying attention daily.

I often tell God at the beginning of the day, "If You want to tell me something today, help me hear." As you pray that, God will honor your request by helping you become more sensitive to Him.

Then make it a habit to ask for God's will and direction on issues you face. Ask and wait for Him to answer. When you feel God's nudge, follow it, even if it seems risky or strange. Just as we can learn to pray more effectively, we can learn to hear more clearly.

Like finding time to pray, listening requires effort. To hear a whisper, we need times of quiet, of reflection, of unhurried interaction with Him. Times when the radio is off, when no television plays in the background, when we can think, pray, and hear. Is it any wonder that those who seem to hear the most have disciplined their lives so they include quiet, reflective time—people like Henri Nouwen or Brennan Manning? Whispers require quietness and attentiveness. You can listen for them in a car, in your study, in a quiet moment at work.

Leaders who are truly connected to the vine make a significant impact on the people they lead and see God's power displayed in and through their congregations. We will only lead with the power turned on if we are personally and intimately connected with the source of power. But that connection isn't only for us personally. We must also pray together for the needs of our flocks.

EMPOWERED PRAYER FOR THE FLOCK

"Again, I tell you," Jesus said, "that if two of you on earth agree about anything you ask for, it will be done for you by my Father in heaven. For where two or three come together in my name, there I am with them" (Matthew 18:19-20). Leaders who invest quality unhurried time in prayer for their congregations understand and believe these biblical truths:

- We can do nothing of lasting spiritual value without the power of Jesus in our midst.
- Jesus eagerly desires to see large amounts of spiritual fruit from our ministries.
- Jesus is ready to grant our requests but does not promise to bless our ministries unless we ask Him to.
- Humble dependence upon Jesus is the mark of mature leaders; they understand that they are not self-sufficient in the spiritual realm.

So prayer is essential, but what should leaders pray about? That may sound like a silly question. However, all of us have found ourselves in prayer meetings that seemed to have little direction and substance. If God truly works when we pray, *what* we pray for takes on even greater significance.

Pray for one another. Strong leadership groups are those that develop community among themselves. So it makes sense that leaders pray specifically for one another's needs, spiritual health and growth, families, and protection from the enemy.

In Ephesians 6:10-20, Paul reminded us that we are engaged in a spiritual war with real spiritual enemies. All the Evil One needs to do to derail the effectiveness of a congregation is to derail the spiritual lives of its leaders. In fact, spiritual leaders are often those most likely to be at spiritual risk for this very reason. We must take seriously the need for spiritual protection, and our prayer for one another becomes the first line of defense against the Enemy.

Praying for one another in a meaningful way requires transparency in our relationships. The more open we are regarding our personal lives (in a safe, confidential setting), the more open we will be about other issues we face as leaders.

Pray for the needs within your congregation. Financial, physical, family, marriage, spiritual, and emotional struggles influence spiritual health. In a small church, it is possible that leaders are fairly aware of a majority of these needs. This will not be the case in a larger church. There, it is important to build prayer networks so everyone who is a regular part of the congregation is prayed for on a periodic basis. In larger churches, the leadership can be the prayer network for key staff and leaders.

Pray for unique missional fulfillment. The two highest callings of the church are to share the good news of Christ with those who do not know Him and to help those who do know Him grow in spiritual maturity. These represent the front and back halves of the Great Commission. However, every congregation has a unique, God-given DNA; congregations have different strengths and different opportunities to fulfill the Great Commission and be involved in discipleship ministries.

Recently, I chatted with a friend who told me of his church's greatest current ministry opportunity: MOPS (Mothers of PreSchoolers). The church of four hundred has sixty moms participating—most from outside the church. Here is a unique ministry opportunity for evangelism with many unchurched mothers.

We know Jesus desires our congregations to bear abundant fruit. We also know He promises to answer prayer when we pray for spiritual fruit. Here are some of the ways we can pray about our churches' role in the Great Commission:

- Lord, help our congregation develop a greater passion for those who don't know You and are without eternal hope.
- Father, we want to be fruitful. Show us ways we can do effective evangelism in our community and among the neighbors and friends of our congregation. Help us understand our unique opportunities to reach people others cannot easily reach.
- Lord, we earnestly desire this congregation to grow in spiritual maturity. Show us ways to help individuals at all levels of spiritual maturity take the next step.
- Father, raise up volunteers with gifts in evangelism and disciple-making whom You can use to pluck spiritual fruit for Your kingdom.

Pray for spiritual renewal. Many of the priorities competing for people's hearts work at cross-purposes with their spiritual health. Intense work pressures, the pursuit of wealth, unhealthy marriages, child-rearing demands, emotional issues, abuse, and other forces work to prevent people from experiencing the full freedom of life in Christ and wholehearted discipleship. It is our privilege to pray that God brings spiritual renewal, such that He becomes their highest priority and the expansion of His kingdom becomes their greatest desire. If we believe God answers prayer and wants His people to be fruitful, we will—like the apostle Paul—pray regularly for the spiritual renewal of those in our congregation.

H. I. BEST PRACTICE

Use one of the prayers from the Old or New Testament to pray for your people as those spiritual leaders (and Jesus) did.

Pray for God's kingdom to come to your community. Can we as church leaders make a difference outside the four walls of our church through prayer? Jesus said yes! Some of the most powerful words He gave us to pray are these: "Our Father in heaven, hallowed be your name, your kingdom come, your will be done on earth as it is in heaven" (Matthew 6:9-10).

Even though we live in a sinful, unjust, corrupt, and harsh world, we are invited and encouraged to pray that God's will would be done. Jesus is inviting us to pray that His kingdom would come to our courthouses, our schoolhouses, our police stations, and our communities and that God's holy, just, loving will would prevail in those places just as completely as it prevails in heaven. It sounds incredible, but Jesus is the one who calls us to this prayer.

What leaders pray for, congregations will begin to pray for. As we pray such radical prayers as these, it is likely that God will start to show members of the congregation ways they can become involved in bringing His kingdom to the marketplace and public arena.

Pray for supernatural and divine wisdom as you lead Christ's congregation on His behalf. Leadership is complicated work. Leaders wade into relational issues and conflicts that will earn them scars; leaders think outside the comfortable box where many within the congregation prefer to live; and leaders call a congregation to follow them to sometimes scary pastures. Furthermore, the church is God's chosen instrument to reach the world. It takes a huge amount of wisdom to know how best to do this—wisdom that ultimately comes from Christ, the vine.

The territory God has called us to take is presently ruled by the Evil One. Spiritual forces are involved. So we need to know God's will and direction to lead wisely. Divine wisdom comes through divine means, and that is appropriated through concerted, regular, serious prayer as the *first* thing, not the *last* thing. Plan great things, think great things, do great things, but above all, pray great things.

H. I. MOMENT

How well is our board doing in finding quality time for strategic prayer?

As a board, we ought to be strategically praying about:

- _Building disciples_____
- _____
- _____
- _____
- _____

When the board discusses this chapter, share your answers.

H. I. BEST PRACTICE

Whenever you as a board are unable to reach consensus (not necessarily unanimity) or do not quite feel that a direction or decision is right, take a time-out and ask God for guidance. Even if it takes additional time outside the meeting, God will answer your prayer and provide direction. We just need to ask — often.

Listen together as you pray. We discussed the importance of listening when spending individual time with God. This applies to corporate prayer as well. As we seek God's will and direction together, we can expect Him to answer. Often that answer takes the form of His gentle impressions on several or all of our hearts. It is amazing to watch God meld hearts as leaders pray together. *We don't shut up*

Learn to be together in prayerful silence, asking God to reveal Himself. It may be awkward at times, but silence is a friend that allows us to hear God's gentle whispers. *We don't worship together*

Worship together as you pray. Combining music, praise, and Scripture helps focus hearts on our Leader and moves our prayers to the next level. Worship facilitates intimacy with Jesus, breaks down barriers between people, humbles hearts before God in dependence, and prepares us to pray and listen.

I know leadership boards that set aside special time monthly or quarterly to worship and pray without time pressure or a business agenda. Board members may invite other staff members or a larger group of church leaders to join them. The group enters into an attitude of praise and worship, interspersing music with Scripture and prayer. They might pray aloud through some of the prayer emphases we've just discussed. Other times the room is quiet as they pray silently, meditate, or experience the presence of God.

If any members believe God has impressed on them an issue to pray for, they do so. And if a member feels God may be trying to communicate direction, he or she will share that "heart impression" to see if others are sensing the same. There is a sense of expectancy that God can, if He so desires, communicate answers or direction as they pray together.

It is a time of worship, of supplication, and of listening to the Spirit of God as a group. Above all, it is a time of humble corporate connection with the Lord of the church, experiencing His presence and acknowledging their dependence.

None of us can remain unchanged after being in the genuine presence of God, and there is a qualitative change both to leaders and the group process when leaders move beyond mere leadership to intimacy with Christ *in* their leadership. While it is a stretch for some in the beginning, this time of intimate corporate prayer quickly becomes one of the most strategic events on the calendar. Those who practice these extended times of worship and prayer report significant spiritual and leadership breakthroughs.

LEADERSHIP WITH THE POWER ON

I am haunted by the picture of that hotel on the banks of the Chao Phraya River: beautiful by day but proven empty by night. I believe this is an accurate picture of leaders who do not remember that fruit comes only from Jesus and is appropriated through prayer. By ourselves, we can develop wonderful facilities and manage great programs, but without the power of the Holy Spirit, we are unable to produce lasting spiritual fruit. When this happens, our ministries are as empty and ineffective as the condemned hotel, no matter how good they look on the outside.

However, leaders who make prayer one of their top leadership priorities see God work in ways they could never have imagined. All because they are relying on and appropriating His supernatural, life-giving, and life-changing power for lasting spiritual fruit. It is our choice. We can lead with the power on or the power off.

H. I. MOMENT

My three greatest "takeaways" from this chapter are:

- _Pray greatly_
- _Shut up!_
- _What is pruning?_

My greatest challenges in getting unhurried time with Jesus are:

- _Work schedule_
-
-

I am going to start asking Christ for greater spiritual fruit in the following areas of my life:

- *Personal obedience*
- *Devotional life*
- _____

For board discussion: We agree to the following commitments regarding our corporate prayer:

- _____
- _____
- _____

H. I. WRAP-UP: KEEPING THE SPIRITUAL POWER HIGH

- Leaders spend unhurried time with God.
- Leaders discover and rediscover His Word.
- Leaders display prayerful, expectant dependence.
- Leaders embrace the hard work of prayer.
- Leaders actively listen to God.
- Leaders pray for one another.
- Leaders pray for the congregation's needs.
- Leaders pray for unique missional fulfillment.
- Leaders pray for spiritual renewal.
- Leaders pray that God's kingdom would come to the community and the world.
- Leaders pray for supernatural and divine wisdom as they lead their congregation.
- Leaders listen corporately to God.
- Leaders worship together.

Chapter Four

SIX-DIMENSIONAL LEADERSHIP, PART TWO

Strategy is important. Leadership is crucial. But strategy and leadership without the power of God will not yield the eternal fruit that Christ has called the church to experience.

The first dimension of Six-Dimensional Leadership is job one for church leaders: keeping themselves and their flocks intimately connected with Jesus, the Head and Lord of the church. All the other leadership dimensions we'll consider in this chapter are subservient to ensuring spiritual power through an ongoing, intimate, organic connection with Jesus. Where intimacy with Christ is not a hallmark of leadership and "the power is not on," the next five dimensions will not move someone toward life change or vibrancy

When connection to Christ is strong, the remaining dimensions of leadership—teaching; protecting; caring; developing, empowering, and releasing; and leading—will contribute to a healthy and vibrant body. Intimacy with Christ combined with these five dimensions can lead a congregation into spiritual health and joyful ministry.

Let's begin by looking at the second of these high-impact leadership dimensions: teaching.

LEADERSHIP DIMENSION TWO: TEACHING

In his book *The Second Coming of the Church*, George Barna shared some of the "street-level theology" that a significant percentage of Americans believe:

- The Bible teaches that God helps those who help themselves (81 percent).
- It doesn't matter what religious faith you follow, because they all teach the same lessons (38 percent).
- All people will experience the same outcome after death, regardless of their religious beliefs (44 percent).
- The Bible teaches that money is the root of all evil (49 percent).
- The Bible is not totally accurate in all that it teaches (34 percent).
- Satan is not a living being, just a symbol of evil (60 percent).
- All people pray to the same god or spirit, no matter what name they use for that spiritual being (53 percent).
- All religious faiths teach equally valid truths (40 percent).
- The most important task in life is taking care of family (56 pecent).
- People are blessed by God so they can enjoy life as much as possible (72 percent).[1]

You probably recognize that not one of these statements is consistent with biblical teaching. Yet many of these beliefs are deeply held by those who walk into our churches today — and in some cases by those who have been in our churches a long time!

A generation ago, there was a fair amount of common Bible knowledge, even among those who were not committed Christians. Today, those coming into our congregations have little understanding of God's truth. If they are going to negotiate life as His people, they need to be taught and be given tools to learn Scripture on their own. Ensuring this happens is a central role of leaders.

The measure of how well we are doing with the teaching task is found in Ephesians 4:11-13:

It was [Christ] who gave some to be apostles, some to be prophets, some to be evangelists, and some to be pastors and teachers, to prepare God's people for works of service, so that the body of Christ may be built up until we all reach unity in the faith and in the knowledge of the Son of God and become mature, attaining to the whole measure of the fullness of Christ.

In this passage, success is determined by the congregation's growing spiritual maturity. Marks of maturity include preparing people for works of service, unity in the body, and a solid understanding of the work of Christ.

God's Word is foundational to everything we are and do as believers. Making sure those in our congregation know the Bible is foundational to equipping believers for "every good work" (2 Timothy 3:14-17). This responsibility is not as simple as it might sound. For instance:

- How many in your congregation have read the entire Bible?
- Is there a systematic effort to teach your congregation the foundational doctrines of the faith?
- Are you helping people from youth through senior adults engage in personal study of Scripture?

Theology, however, is not enough. People need to be drawn into an abiding relationship with Jesus that ensures a lasting impact on their families, careers, ministries, and lives. The key is to help people understand how to apply the principles of God's Word so they become mature in both their love for Him and their life with Him.

Targeted teaching. If the target of our teaching is spiritual maturity, as Ephesians 4:11-13 declares, it is vital for leaders to define what spiritual maturity looks like from a biblical perspective. Willow Creek Community Church in South Barrington, Illinois, has defined spiritual maturity—its target—through what it calls the "Five Gs." In broad strokes, the following Gs draw the "essential marks of someone devoted to Christ and His Church."[2]

- Grace: People understand and have received Christ's saving grace.

- Growth: People are intentionally pursuing spiritual growth.
- Groups: People are connected with others and are growing together.
- Gifts: People are discovering, developing, and using their spiritual gifts.
- Good Stewardship: People are tithing their resources back to God.

Your definition of maturity may differ from Willow Creek's; that's fine. The point is to *have* a definition. Without a target, you and your congregation will never know if you are hitting the mark. We can close our eyes and hope the end results of our ministries are mature disciples, but unless we are clear about what a disciple looks like and are willing to examine the results, we are most likely fooling ourselves.

H. I. MOMENT

Do we as leaders have a definition of what a mature Christ follower looks like?

If we do, is this definition well known by our people?

If we don't, what are some key characteristics of a mature Christ follower?

- Honors God's word and follows it
-
-
-
-
-

Does my life reflect these characteristics?

Helping people test-drive truth. After we know our target, our teaching is only completed when our congregations put into practice what they've learned. After all, our goal is not to produce knowledge-rich brains but practice-rich lives that flow from a deep love of Jesus. This means we need to go the last mile by providing the challenge and opportunity for people to practice what they are taught—to test-drive what they learn.

Andy Stanley challenged his congregation to test-drive truth when he taught about using resources to advance the kingdom. After preaching that everything we have belongs to God, each person at North Point Community Church in Alpharetta, Georgia, received a sealed envelope containing money—fives, tens, and twenties—totaling $37,000 in all. Each envelope came with a card reading, "I'm going to invest in God's kingdom by _____." Congregants were to use the money outside the church and report back on how they had invested in God's kingdom. The church gathered thousands of responses, and Stanley estimates their $37,000 probably grew to a half-million-dollar investment in kingdom causes.[3]

Stanley invited his congregation to test-drive the truth of what he had preached. With this church-wide experiment, they realized the joy of obedience and experienced the truth of God's ownership of all their possessions.

The proof of learning is not a changed intellect but a transformed character. Character changes when we start to practice biblical habits. New habits are formed when we are challenged to dip our big toe into that truth and test the waters.

H. I. MOMENT

Can we identify specific ways we have encouraged our congregation to test-drive truth in the past year?

- _____
- _____
- _____

How can we begin to take test-drives more often?

LEADERSHIP DIMENSION THREE: PROTECTING

The third dimension of high-impact leadership is protecting. Paul's instructions to the elders on a coastal beach in Ephesus help us understand why protection of a congregation is so important:

> Keep watch over yourselves and all the flock of which the Holy Spirit has made you overseers. Be shepherds of the church of God, which he bought with his own blood. I know that after I leave, savage wolves will come in among you and will not spare the flock. Even from your own number men will arise and distort the truth in order to draw away disciples after them. So be on your guard! (Acts 20:28-31)

Paul told these leaders that their responsibilities would include dealing with situations threatening the flock. This did not surprise them and should not surprise us. Every local church has an enemy — the Evil One — who will do all he can to disrupt, hurt, and destroy the unity and lives of God's people.

Against what are leaders charged to protect their congregations?

- Teaching that is contrary to the Scriptures and that leads individuals down a path that will harm them (see Acts 20:28-31)
- Situations where a member of the congregation is engaged in obvious, ongoing sin (see 1 Corinthians 5)
- People who are causing division in the body — whether out of a need for power, a doctrinal "hobby horse," or divisive attitudes (see Romans 16:17-19; 2 Timothy 3:1-5; Titus 3:10-11)

A Leadership Fable

Allow me to share a fable with you that illustrates a flock under attack.

Pastor Bill moved to Pennsylvania to plant a church. Soon after, staff members from the larger mother church stopped by for a visit. "We're really praying for you," they said before they left.

At first Bill assumed they were simply praying for ministry success. Soon, though, he began to realize they knew something he didn't. Bill noticed that Chris, a founding member of the new church and a board member, seemed to have veto power on board decisions. He also noted that when the board made decisions Chris didn't like, their confidential discussions became common knowledge among Chris's friends in the congregation—a violation of board policy. These friends would then lobby Bill and others to move in a different direction.

Over several years, elder/board meetings became increasingly difficult and sometimes downright ugly. The language and attitudes from several of the members shocked Bill. As Chris moved in on relationships, some board members who had been Bill's close supporters became distant and critical. Bill came to dread board meetings after being targeted on numerous issues. He could only conclude that his leadership was slowly but surely being undermined.

The church was growing rapidly, and though most members had little idea of the pain behind the scenes, Bill became increasingly discouraged. He saw Chris as an arsonist who lit fires all over the church but was never around when the firemen came to extinguish them.

Soon, a group of dissidents headed by Chris wanted Bill to leave. At a congregational meeting, after a vote of overwhelming support for Bill, one dissident loudly stated he was going to withdraw all of his financial support. He then stalked out of the auditorium.

Bill started to question the pastors at the mother church and discovered Chris had a problematic history there as well. In fact, that pastor had vowed Chris would never serve in leadership there again! Chris and his friends eventually left Bill's church, but they continued sowing seeds of discord and dissention among friends and acquaintances still there.

After time, Bill and his wife made the painful decision to leave. His board was not ready to place the two main dissidents under discipline, although board members had been strongly encouraged to do so by many from whom they sought counsel. Bill left, discouraged and clinically depressed.

The congregation grew increasingly aware of the underlying power struggles. In response to Bill's leaving and the lack of resolution to those power plays, more than half of the congregation left after a series of congregational meetings — even as Chris returned and reclaimed a leadership role.

A new pastor was called, and he was out of the ministry within a few years. A third pastor was called. He, too, left amid power issues after a few years. Finally, the local bishop intervened, insisting Chris could no longer serve in any leadership position.

The church had torn up three pastors and left numerous wounded members in its wake. One person who watched the destruction observed this church had hurt more people than it helped.

How many of us have watched similar situations where leaders have not had the courage to confront toxic, divisive individuals who wound the sheep and divide the flock of Christ? One of the primary roles of a shepherd is to protect the flock from harm. David actually fought lions to protect his flock, but leaders are often unwilling to confront divisive individuals who do as much damage as a lion loose among the sheep!

We cannot know what we prevent. Only what we fail to prevent

Handling Conflict

Al is gone. What did that prevent? Deb Quant, Paula Hoover, Don Klattke, etc

The need to protect our congregations *will* occur, even in churches with the most attentive shepherds. So how we handle the accompanying conflict is important.

You are likely familiar with the scriptural principles found in Matthew 18; 1 Corinthians 5; 2 Corinthians 2:5-11; and Galatians 6:1-2. We are to start the conversations gently and with prayer in the hope that we can persuade those causing harm to move away from their sin. If this is not successful, we are to apply successive steps of pressure, always seeking resolution and a restoration to fellowship. When all else fails, Scripture calls for the individual to be put out of the body — again, with the hope that this action will cause him or her to turn back to God. All confrontation is to be done in love accompanied by firmness.

Yet even though we know the biblical process, we prefer to sidestep it. Most people do not like conflict and confrontation (beware of those who do). And we live in a day of political correctness, where it is not

Hating it and doing it ~~better it~~ anyway is better than Hating it and not doing it, or loving it and doing it.

popular to label behavior as "wrong" or to "judge" others. None of us signs up for leadership with the hope that we'll get to deal with sinful people and ugly situations.

The question we must ask is: "Do we love God's flock as much as He does?" When we confront false teaching, sinful behavior, or division, we are acting on His behalf and obeying His command to protect His sheep. Are we willing to put up with momentary discomfort in order to protect people for whom Jesus was willing to die? These difficult confrontations are an unwelcome but necessary part of the leadership calling.

Principles for Dealing with Difficult People

When you lead with the power on, you can move into these unwelcome situations with assurance that you are not alone; the Shepherd is guiding every step of the way. He has also given key principles to keep in mind.

- Examine your motives to ensure your true concern is the health and protection of God's flock (see Galatians 6:1-2).
- Be gentle but firm (see Galatians 6:1).
- Follow the successive steps of Matthew 18:15-20 with the goal of restoration.
- Do everything you can to bring the individual back to a place of fellowship with the body.
- Where it might be helpful, bring in a third party, who can mediate and bring understanding between warring parties (see Matthew 18:16).
- Consider training your leaders in conflict resolution, to heighten chances of a preferred solution.
- While you cannot judge motives, you can judge behavior. Paul made it clear in his pastoral epistles that some behaviors should be called illegal in the church, and those who practice them should be dealt with firmly and swiftly (see Romans 16:17-19; 2 Timothy 3:1-5; and Titus 3:10-11). Not to do so is to allow the flock of Jesus to be wounded and His body made sick.

LEADERSHIP DIMENSION FOUR: CARING

Love among believers has been a hallmark of the church since the beginning. We read, for instance, this account of the early church: "All the believers were together and had everything in common. Selling their possessions and goods, they gave to anyone as he had need" (Acts 2:44-45). The apostle John called love the defining signature quality of believers. This love prompts the fourth of the six leadership dimensions: caring. Consider John's statement in 1 John 3:16-18:

> This is how we know what love is: Jesus Christ laid down his life for us. And we ought to lay down our lives for our brothers. If anyone has material possessions and sees his brother in need but has no pity on him, how can the love of God be in him? Dear children, let us not love with words or tongue but with actions and in truth.

Caring for individual and family needs within our congregations is God-honoring—and time-consuming. We usually can't apply a quick fix when a marriage is in trouble. A family in financial difficulty may need both immediate help and long-term financial counseling. Severe illness will require an ongoing plan for providing support. Similarly, helping those with deep emotional issues requires patience and love.

As you consider how to ensure members receive care in times of need, consider four opportunities that will allow everyone in the congregation to learn how to love in a Jesus way.

Develop care teams. Rather than the board taking primary responsibility for dealing with personal needs, consider developing a team of people with the gifts of mercy and caring. It didn't take the early church long to figure out it could not do everything. One of the first organizational decisions it made was to appoint individuals "full of the Spirit and wisdom" to organize care for the needy (Acts 6:1-7).

Train the congregation to notice needs and respond personally. If love is the signature quality of believers, we should invite people to become experts in loving one another. Our individualistic culture trains us not to ask for help or look for people with personal needs. Yet Jesus wants us to help people develop an internal radar system that notices needs that can be met within the body.

Build safety nets. Incorporating safety nets into your ministry provides contexts in which to identify and meet needs. Because we are most likely to become aware of needs in the context of relationship, these safety nets will most often be linked to the church's relational networks. Small groups, for instance, become a place where deeper relationships can develop and people can open up about their challenges. As you train leaders in various ministries, ask them to be aware of needs within their group and to encourage group members to meet those needs.

Practice proactive care. Congregations the world over encounter common issues: marriage difficulties, child-rearing concerns, financial stresses, emotional challenges. Rather than dealing with these issues one at a time, develop classes or small groups to address them before they become problems. Train qualified individuals to mentor people who are struggling in specific areas. Watch for trends in your church and community that indicate deep, widespread issues where the church can speak and offer encouragement and assistance (for example, divorce, unemployment, and loneliness).

The best care plan will challenge the whole congregation to become lovers of one another, ask qualified volunteers to develop teams of caregivers, and address known issues proactively with biblical training. Develop love as a signature quality of your congregation, and it will be infectious.

H. I. MOMENT

Take two minutes and jot down your thoughts on the care system your church currently has in place.

- _____

- _____

- _____
- _____
- _____

LEADERSHIP DIMENSION FIVE: DEVELOPING, EMPOWERING, AND RELEASING

Excellent parable

Consider this strategy for fighting a war: A volunteer militia is rigorously recruited and offered a weekly one-hour seminar on how to fight a battle. In the workshop, the battalion commander tells great war stories and gives advice on combat strategy. After a few years of seminars, the militia is told to get into the battle. Some try. Casualties are high. A few drop out. A fraction with natural battle skills say, "I like this," and charge into combat. Most volunteers decide they need more seminars (and that the seminar room is *much* safer than the foxhole).

As crazy as such a strategy sounds, tens of thousands of churches around the world follow variations on it; it's their version of "equipping and deploying" believers. The result? Those troops not already wounded are still participating in seminars and rarely engaged in battle.

One of the greatest ministry challenges today is ensuring people are equipped for ministry and then deployed to minister in meaningful ways. This is our responsibility as leaders. Let's review some scriptural truths:

1. The Holy Spirit has given every believer a spiritual gift or gifts: "We have different gifts, according to the grace given us" (Romans 12:6-8; see also 1 Corinthians 12:12-31).
2. God has assigned every believer a unique contribution to the advancement of His kingdom: "For we are God's workmanship, created in Christ Jesus to do good works, which God prepared in advance for us to do" (Ephesians 2:10). The word *workmanship* comes from a Greek word meaning "work of art." Each of us is specifically designed by God to make the unique contribution He has prepared for us.

3. The body is not whole unless all members are using their God-given gifts: "Now to each one the manifestation of the Spirit is given for the *common good.* . . . The body is a *unit*, though it is made up of many parts; and though all its parts are many, they form one body" (1 Corinthians 12:1-26, emphasis added). To the extent people are using their gifts, the church will be healthy and congregations will make the impact God intends.

4. One primary responsibility of a leader is to see that people are developed, empowered, and released: "It was [Christ] who gave some to be apostles, some to be prophets, some to be evangelists, and some to be pastors and teachers, *to prepare God's people for works of service*, so that the body of Christ may be built up" (Ephesians 4:11-12, emphasis added).

Teaching is not enough. God has specifically tasked us to develop and release people on His behalf. After years of assuming this happens automatically, we now know the osmosis approach is a nonstarter. An intentional strategy for equipping and deploying is the only way we will realize the biblical vision of the total body involved in life-changing, community-influencing, kingdom-building ministry.

Our task of developing, equipping, and releasing means helping people identify their spiritual gifts and mentoring them as they develop those gifts.

Identifying spiritual gifts. As we watch growing believers in our congregations, what giftings do we see? Someone who is always coming to another's aid and comfort probably has gifts of mercy and care. The one who can organize absolutely anything, the gift of administration; the one who can make Scripture come alive and motivate people to follow the Word, the gift of teaching. One way to scope out some of these gifts is to periodically ask staff members and volunteers to identify any person whose gift really stands out—whether in a ministry or personal setting.

In a congregation of fewer than three hundred, it is possible to identify many people's gifts by watching closely and involving your staff members and key ministry leaders. As congregations grow past three hundred, identification will usually require a more systematic approach.

After we've noticed people's gifting, we'll also need a plan for equipping them to use those gifts in ministry.

Equipping through mentoring. For too long, the church has hired professionals to do the work of ministry when its biblical job description is "to prepare God's people for works of service, so that the body of Christ may be built up" (Ephesians 4:12).

Jesus equipped the disciples through the mentoring model. By spending time with them, giving them limited ministry opportunities before large ones, and then providing feedback, He prepared them for the time when they would lead the church. We also see the multiplication principle at work in the early church. As a new believer, Paul was mentored by Barnabas. Later, Paul enjoined one of those he mentored, Timothy, to "entrust" what he had been taught "to reliable men who will also be qualified to teach others" (2 Timothy 2:2). We will never make a profound difference in our ministries until we think "multiplication" in everything we do. Multiplication starts with mentoring and training others.

At every ministry level, we ought to be mentoring one or more for that ministry. This means that both lay and professional practitioners need training so they can mentor well. Mentoring can be as simple as Sunday-school teachers inviting potential teachers to teach with them or as intentional as training small-group leaders in the dynamics of small-group leadership.

Larry Osborne, pastor of North Coast Church, a congregation of more than six thousand in Vista, California, insists his staff members multiply themselves. To set the pace, he has others share preaching responsibilities with him. The result is that North Coast Church has trained leaders—actually a bench of upcoming leaders—at every level of ministry. Larry believes in multiplication!

Jesus wants to free His children for maximum impact with the gifts He has generously given. God's people are not whole unless they understand how He has gifted them and are actively serving Him. In addition, the church is whole and healthy to the extent that people are engaged together in meaningful ministry.

H. I. MOMENT

Is the "developing, empowering, and releasing" strategy for our congregation intentional or accidental? Why?

LEADERSHIP DIMENSION SIX: LEADING

The final dimension of high-impact leadership is . . . leading. That may seem self-evident, but there is a debate today in the church over the nature of leadership: Are pastors and church leaders called to *shepherd* or *lead* their congregations?

Those who choose "shepherd" believe that if we pray and teach the Word, everything else falls into place. Taking the picture of the Old Testament shepherd as the model, there is a sense of "being with the sheep" but not "leading the sheep." Taken to the extreme, advocates of this position reject leadership notions of planning, strategy, evaluation, and vision. Significant voices on the other side champion strong, intentional, directional leadership that challenges the congregation to take as much territory for God as possible. Taken to the extreme, advocates of this position can emphasize "hard" business principles over "soft" spiritual principles. *When has GCR been? Where is it mostly?*

This is not merely a debate among pastors. Both positions are often represented on leadership boards: Some board members emphasize prayer and some emphasize strategic thinking—both to accomplish ministry objectives.

What does the Bible say about this question? The shepherding metaphor is the most familiar one there. Yet Scripture passages related to church leaders indicate that intentional leadership is also expected. In 1 Peter 5:1-4, leaders are called to oversee the flock. Some of Paul's letters were directed to two men he was mentoring as pastors: Timothy and Titus. In his instructions, he encouraged them to preach without apology, to pray constantly, to confront false teaching and divisive men, to mentor and train faithful men, and to appoint godly individuals to leadership. These are clearly leadership tasks! The impression we have of Timothy is that he was not a natural-born leader, but Paul exhorted him to take up his responsibility to lead — even if it was outside his comfort zone.

I believe the resolution to the question of "shepherd" or "lead" can be found in understanding that we come to the leadership task from differing perspectives. I call the two ends of this leadership spectrum "spiritualists" and "strategists." A spiritualist will emphasize dependence on God while a strategist focuses on intentional actions and living.

The *spiritualist* on a church board or staff is the one who strongly identifies with the need to appropriate God's power through prayer — sometimes to the exclusion of planning and strategy. Moses is a good example of a spiritualist. Prayer was his default when faced with difficulty. He loved nothing more than to be in the presence of his Lord, and God rewarded that desire by meeting with him face-to-face (see Exodus 33:11). After the incident with the golden calf, Moses was so concerned that God's presence go with the Israelites that he pled with God to remain with the people even in the face of their egregious sin (see Exodus 33:12-23).

Strategy was less of a gift for Moses. In fact, he nearly burned out from trying to deal personally with the issues of several million people! Jethro, his father-in-law, had to help Moses develop a strategy for organizing the people and arbitrating their disputes.

On the other end of the spectrum, the *strategist* is someone who loves to plan, think ahead, set goals, evaluate results, question practices, and insist on "ministry results." These individuals are sometimes impatient with the spiritualists who, in their opinion, are simply unwilling to use their God-given abilities to think strategically. What's more, to a strategist, a spiritualist seems to think naïvely that God is going to do everything without much effort from us.

I believe Paul tended toward the strategist end of the spectrum. On his missionary journeys, he thought carefully about where to plant churches and chose the population centers of the Roman Empire, where the gospel would have the greatest impact. As he planted churches, he was intentional about appointing leaders and mentoring pastors. In evangelism, he strategically tailored his message so his audience would understand and respond to the gospel (see 1 Corinthians 9:22-23).

This does not mean that Paul was not also deeply spiritual or a man of great prayer. But he tended to look at his ministry from a strategic perspective. At times the Holy Spirit had to use a two-by-four to get his attention when he was moving in the wrong direction (see Acts 16:6-10).

As you might imagine, a strategist and a spiritualist will face challenges as they work together in leadership. Differing leadership bents may well have been at the core of the rift between Paul and Barnabas over John Mark (see Acts 15:36-41). Paul, with his strategist bent, grew impatient with John Mark and was blinded to the benefits he brought to the work. Barnabas, whose name means "encourager," was probably much less bent toward the strategic than toward the relational and spiritual. Barnabas had a more understanding approach. He took leave of Paul and took John Mark under his wing. Later in life, Paul exhibited a softer attitude toward John Mark, and it is clear that they reconciled their relationship (see 2 Timothy 4:11).

If Paul and Barnabas could stumble on relational shoals over their differing approaches to life and ministry, it should not surprise us that we face these challenges as we lead together. Apart from Christ, who was a perfect balance between the spiritualist and the strategist, all of us fall somewhere on a continuum toward one side or the other. We do not see life perfectly, and we have been gifted differently—but we need each other.

A great example of spiritualists and strategists' need for each other is found in the book of Nehemiah. Ezra had brought a remnant of the exiled Israelites back to Jerusalem and, from all accounts, was an effective spiritual leader. However, Ezra seemed not to have had many strategic bones in his body. Once back home, the people quickly fell into deep discouragement and disorganization due to the ruins of the city and the lack of security from surrounding enemies.

God finally raised up Nehemiah, a man deeply gifted in action, intentionality, and strategy, to come to Jerusalem and single-handedly bring organization and security to the city. Nehemiah was not only focused and mission driven ("Get the wall repaired"), he also was nobody's fool and was not in the least intimidated by the taunting and schemes of their enemies.

Which of these men did God need? Both! God used Ezra to bring the people back and provide spiritual direction. But God used Nehemiah to solve a critical problem.

This applies to the question of which is right, the spiritualist or the strategist. Biblically, both are. Those who advocate for one pole or the other fail to understand the genius of "and." Leadership is prayer *and* strategy. It is following Christ *and* applying the best of our thinking on behalf of His kingdom. It is passionate dependence *and* ferocious resolve.

Why, then, do we tend to polarize the question rather than see it holistically? I believe we do so because we are more comfortable operating out of our personal paradigm and want to view that paradigm as right.

We ought to thank God for both the spiritualists, who remind us to trust God and live in dependence, and the strategists, who prompt us to think strategically for the advancement of His kingdom. When we understand that both of these approaches are biblical, and that it is in the balance of deep dependence and ferocious resolve that the best ministry happens, then we will embrace both and denigrate neither. God has gifted us differently, and it is in the plurality of gifting that we are most complete.

H. I. MOMENT

Where do you fall on the spiritualist/strategist continuum?

Spiritualist   Strategist

----◆--◆----

Together with the rest of your board (or staff team), discuss where people see themselves on the spiritualist/strategist continuum and whether this is how others see them.

When might disagreements or conflicts among team members have been the result of these differences?

Leadership styles. Another truth in this equation is that leadership looks different in different people. There is no one perfect leadership style. There are vastly different styles even among strong, wise, visionary leaders. For instance, Bill Hybels, senior pastor of Willow Creek Community Church, points out ten identifiable leadership styles. Note how you see elements of both spiritualists and strategists in this list.

- *Visionary.* Carries a crystal-clear picture of what needs to happen and recruits others to the dream. Idealistic, black and white. Will die for the vision.
- *Directional.* Uncanny ability to choose the right path for an organization when it reaches a critical intersection. Can sort through options based on an organization's purpose, values, personnel, and opportunities.
- *Strategic.* Ability to break an exciting vision down to sequential, advisable steps. Tries to get components of a team to work together.
- *Managing.* Ability to organize people, processes, resources, and systems to achieve vision.
- *Motivational.* Ability to keep teammates inspired. Overcomes tiredness, low morale, discouragement, apathy, and fogginess.
- *Shepherding.* Slowly builds a team. Loves them deeply and draws them into community so that mission is accomplished through commitment to each other.
- *Team-building.* Can recruit, develop the right people for the right positions, and turn them loose to lead. Driven by vision, strategy, and correct placement of personnel.

- *Entrepreneur.* Exemplifies any of the preceding styles but functions best in a start-up mode. High energy, creative, easily bored, looks for challenge.
- *Reengineering.* Creates a turnaround environment, renews vision and focus, revitalizes organizations. Takes a consulting approach.
- *Bridge-building.* Builds alliances to achieve mission. Flexible, skilled in negotiating and achieving compromises, loves a wide variety of people and a complex environment.[4]

What is strong leadership? It could be any one of these styles. We ought to embrace, appreciate, and accept the many-sided facets of leadership styles rather than assume our favorite is the best one.

H. I. MOMENT

Identify the leadership style that best describes you:_____.

As a board or staff team, ask team members to identify their leadership styles; then, discuss how these styles can either create tension for others who lead differently or, if understood, contribute to a stronger team.

Name_____Style_____
Name_____Style_____
Name_____Style_____
Name_____Style_____
Name_____Style_____
Name_____Style_____
Name_____Style_____
Name_____Style_____

EMPOWERED SHEPHERDS

No matter what our leadership style or bent, the term "shepherd" is always an active metaphor for church leaders. The shepherd of the ancient world was a leader to his sheep. He fed them, protected them from harm, cared for them, found the strays, and led them to water and pasture (see Psalm 23). A good shepherd led his flock with tenderness, kindness, and compassion.

Just as the sheep are led to the right pastures, so congregations are led to the places where they will be healthy and productive for God's kingdom. Through teaching, care, protecting, and equipping "with the power on," leaders shepherd congregations to specific places where healthy growth and ministry occur. This is intentional rather than accidental leadership. It comes from fully dimensional leaders who determine, with appropriate input from and communication with the congregation, who the church is, why it exists, where it is going, and what it does next.

H. I. MOMENT

Does our leadership board have a job description that reflects the biblical dimensions of leadership God gave His leaders?

Of the six leadership dimensions outlined in chapters 3 and 4, quickly rate the strength of each dimension of leadership in your church with a number from 1 to 10 (10 being the strongest).

____Ensuring spiritual power
____Teaching
____Protecting
____Caring
____Developing, empowering, and releasing
____Leading

Are there any dimensions to which you need to give specific attention?

H. I. WRAP-UP: SIX-DIMENSIONAL LEADERSHIP

1. Ensuring spiritual power
2. Teaching
3. Protecting
4. Caring
5. Developing, empowering, and releasing
6. Leading

Chapter Five

DECIPHERING THE GENETIC CODE OF YOUR CHURCH

Every congregation carries a unique genetic code. The code is a complex combination of the church's history, philosophy of ministry, pastors and leaders, conflicts and resolutions, congregational makeup (ethnically, socially, and economically), and a host of other factors. These factors combine to explain why a congregation is what it is and operates as it does.

Churches are immensely complex organisms. The better that leaders understand the genetic code of their church, the better they are able to capitalize on its strengths and deal with its weaknesses.

THE STORY OF FAITH CHURCH: A CASE STUDY

Faith Church started thirty years ago in a Chicago suburb (church name and location have been changed). The philosophy of the founding members was that Faith would never grow beyond 250 people. This philosophy partly grew out of a desire for a family atmosphere and partly out of a commitment to plant other churches. To ensure this guideline "stuck," an architect was instructed to design a facility that could not easily be expanded. (I give Faith's leaders credit for making decisions consistent with their philosophy!)

Over the years, Faith helped start a number of churches, but Faith also continued to grow—to five hundred, at its peak. The congregation considered relocating twice during its first twenty years, but the decision was controversial, given the church's original philosophy. The congregation stepped back from this decision both times in order to avoid conflict.

Some years ago, many in the body grew restless about their inability to have greater ministry impact. So the church established a vision committee to consider Faith's mission and future. The committee, led by a trained facilitator from outside the church, included new and former leaders as well as a cross-section of members.

This decision quickly became controversial. In fact, soon after the vision committee made recommendations to the congregation, major conflict broke out.

The committee had made three key recommendations. First, it strongly recommended Faith transition from being an inward-looking church primarily concerned with those in the congregation to an outward-looking church with a strong evangelistic emphasis. And the committee established a target of five hundred new believers for the next decade.

Second, the committee issued a strong call for Faith to develop greater dependence on God for ministry results. Many acknowledged that Faith had relied too much on its own gifts, energy, and money and too little on the power of the Holy Spirit.

Finally, the committee recommended establishing a task force to determine whether the congregation should expand on the current campus or look for a new location. This task force (composed of both newer and older church members) concluded it did not make sense to expand on the current property; the group recommended the congregation look for land for future relocation.

Conflict occurred over three major issues. Dissenters felt it was unbiblical to pray for a specific number of converts, so this goal should not be in the vision statement. They complained the church should not relocate even though the congregation had overwhelmingly voted to do just that. Finally, they charged that leadership had taken way too much prerogative in these matters, robbing members of the "congregational" nature of their polity—even though the congregation had specifically debated and voted on each decision.

Church leadership held numerous meetings with those who were unhappy, trying to resolve differences, but to no avail. Eventually the dissenting group tried to force the resignation of the pastor and the board. When the congregation defeated these motions after two difficult meetings, the dissenters walked out, never to return. The group included several of the church's founding members.

Unfortunately, this true story is a variation of many similar stories of many churches. While it is an account of human beings who often violate the unity of the church (it has been happening since Paul wrote to the Corinthians), it is also a story of how the DNA of this church fed the problem.

WHAT HAPPENED HERE?

Nothing that happens in a church takes place in a vacuum. At Faith, many factors related to its genetic code and its history coalesced to explain the conflict and its unfortunate outcome. This story isn't one of the "good guys" and the "bad guys." Despite some ungodly actions and attitudes, Faith's story is primarily one of its particular genetic code.

The concerns about new converts and complaints about relocating were actually fueled by dissent over vision. Faith was founded by leaders thinking family and small church. At five hundred members, a church is no longer small, but some at Faith still thought of it as small. They were dismayed and threatened that Faith was ready to embrace and even facilitate additional growth. The real issue was not whether it was right to pray for five hundred new believers but that such a vision meant Faith was rejecting the family nature of the original founders. The decision to purchase land to relocate was further proof that Faith was moving away from its original vision.

The charge that leadership had taken too much prerogative was based on dynamics that had been in play for years. While elected leadership at Faith had changed over the years, some of the founding members still had significant influence. Several of these people, though not in leadership, had retained unofficial veto power over decisions made by elected board members. Now, even though these individuals tried to exercise their veto, the board—convinced the church needed to move into a new future with a new vision—did not blink as it had in the past.

This meant the rules were changing. While Faith was congregational in nature, it had been careful not to make decisions that would create conflict with those who had unofficial influence. Thus, Faith had twice backed away from relocating. This time, even though the congregation overwhelmingly backed the recommendations, the dissident group thought it was within its rights to fight the decisions and, when all else failed, tried to force a change in elected leadership and the senior pastor.

The dissidents were correct in their fear that the nature of leadership at Faith had changed. In its early existence, Faith had chosen leaders by lot and had not vested them with much authority. This meant, in practice, that those with unofficial influence could claim—with some justification—that leadership did not have the authority to make certain decisions. As the years passed, however, the board started to lead with greater conviction and courage. The congregation accepted this leadership and started to follow. The true influence was now being vested in those elected to lead.

Most church conflict revolves around one of two issues: power and unresolved relational issues. At Faith, while many issues floated around, the real issue was that of power: Who was vested with the power to make critical directional decisions? Certain founding fathers, unwilling to give up their original vision and realizing that their informal veto power was not working this time, precipitated a crisis within the church to prevent the rules from changing. When it became clear that the rules had irrevocably changed, they chose to leave rather than submit to the will of the current majority.

Most pieces of Faith's genetic code were not immediately understood by those in leadership. It took some time for Faith's leaders to understand that the conflict came from dynamics that were strongly entrenched in Faith's history—how it had historically viewed elected leadership, how it had resolved (or not resolved) conflict, its vision of what the church should look like, and its willingness to allow persons of strong influence to determine its direction. Faith's story is a lesson in the tenacious nature of a church's DNA.

UNDERSTANDING YOUR CONGREGATION'S DNA

As church leaders, the better we understand what makes our congregation unique, the wiser our leadership can be. In addition, as we become aware of unhealthy traits within our congregation's past or present, we can address these areas and lead the congregation toward greater health. Lack of understanding leaves us vulnerable to repeat mistakes or to misunderstand issues we face as leaders. Here are a number of questions to explore as you try to understand your congregation's genetic code:

- What do you know about the founding of your church? How do you think the motives and attitudes present in the church's founding—positive or negative—affect the church today?
- What was the philosophy of those who started your congregation? Is it the same today, or has there been a significant shift in mission, vision, or ministry philosophy? How did this shift happen?
- How do people in the church navigate disagreements? Would you give your congregation high or low marks for handling conflict? Do you see patterns here?
- Are you aware of any significant unresolved issues within your congregation? What are they, and why do you think they have not been resolved?
- How would you evaluate the unity of your leadership board? Does your board have a history of unity and love, even when faced with differences, or is there a history of conflict and broken relationships?
- If your congregation faced significant periods of conflict in the past, what do you know about these periods? Is it possible to see trends in either the causes or how the conflict was handled?

- When you consider leadership, now or historically, who has the major influence? Does the church board allow any individual (elected leaders or nonelected persons of influence) veto power over decisions made by the board or congregation? How has the power and influence structure of the church changed over the years?
- Think about major changes the congregation has made, whether related to ministry philosophy, location, ministries, or staff. Does the congregation respond to suggested changes easily, with great resistance — or somewhere in between?
- As you have read this chapter, what genetic issues came to mind? Can you identify where the various pieces came from?
- Are there any subjects, people, or situations related to the ministry of your church that are off-limits for discussion? If so, why do you think these "elephants in the room" cannot be named?

H. I. MOMENT

Walk through these questions as a board, perhaps using a whiteboard. If your discussion surfaces problematic issues, record them and keep them in mind as you read the rest of the chapter.

HEALTHY AND UNHEALTHY DNA

Healthy characteristics of your congregation should be celebrated and affirmed. Your church may have a great reputation for caring for the needs of its community. Celebrate this wonderful biblical strength. Your people may be extraordinarily generous, financially and personally. Thank them and celebrate this generosity. The more you affirm, the more a congregation will recognize its strengths and desire to do even more. We cannot do enough to affirm God's people where they are living in His will.

Leaders should specialize in understanding the strengths of their congregations, in order to affirm them and for ministry effectiveness. As a general rule, it is far easier to build on strengths than to fix weaknesses. Help your people understand and celebrate their strengths, and then help them build on those strengths for even greater ministry impact.

H. I. MOMENT

How often do we find ways as leaders to affirm healthy characteristics within our congregation?

Is this something we need to be more intentional about?

Along with its strengths, every congregation also has unhealthy DNA. Leaders must understand where the congregation is unhealthy, even if they choose not to attack the issue head-on.

It is my conclusion that after bad theology, poor relationships are the next greatest contributor to deadly DNA in the body. It is not surprising that some of the most unhealthy genetics congregations face are in the area of relationships—building and maintaining healthy relationships require a great deal of energy.

Paul regularly addressed the importance of good relationships in his letters to the early church. His epistles contain thirty-four references to "one another": We are to love one another, care for one another, rejoice with one another, forgive one another, teach one another, share with one another, submit to one another, suffer with one another—and on and on. Paul correctly understood that love for one another and the numerous ramifications of that love are the natural outcomes of the true love of Christ and the proof of Christ's work among believers.

How do you measure healthy relationships in a congregation? Consider the following biblical characteristics as you think about your church:

- People care for one another in tangible ways.
- When people fall into sin, friends surround them and lovingly but firmly encourage repentance and change.

- People still love one another when there are disagreements.
- People handle their conflict in a Matthew 18 manner.
- Leaders teach biblical principles for conflict resolution and outline those expectations for the congregation.
- The church culture fosters forgiving quickly and not holding grudges.
- Healthy relationships are encouraged and reinforced at all levels of church ministry, including from the pulpit.
- A high level of trust prevails between the congregation and elected leaders.
- The church lacks factions or power bases.

If bad relationships are a hallmark of unhealthy DNA, the converse is also true: Almost anything is possible in a body that has healthy, God-honoring relationships.

H. I. BEST PRACTICE

Help your congregation understand and adopt the Matthew 18 mind-set for dealing with relational issues. Embed this mind-set by teaching and then insisting that where believers have an issue with one another, they must first talk to that individual before talking to others, including church staff members or leaders.

HEALTHY RELATIONSHIPS ARE MODELED BY LEADERS

We have all learned ways of relating with people from our families of origin—some healthy, some not. Like families, congregations reinforce healthy or unhealthy relationships by what they teach and allow, and particularly by what leaders model. This places a heavy responsibility on leaders to practice what they desire the congregation to practice and to avoid what they want the congregation to avoid.

My observation as a pastor, board member, and consultant in scores of churches is that leaders often get what they deserve from their congregations. Congregations that are relating poorly are often merely following the example of church leaders who do not live by godly principles.

They are more interested in getting their way than submitting in humility to one another. Unity in the church starts with unity on the board, and board unity is a result of declaring some behaviors "illegal."

Board covenants are a way of clarifying what is acceptable and what is unacceptable in leadership relationships — the rules of engagement by which we will live as leaders.

H. I. MOMENT

Stop! Before you continue, which of the practices outlined in this covenant does your board either practice or violate? If some of these practices are violated on a regular basis, what is the result for the board? Much church conflict could be avoided if leadership groups agreed to live in a manner consistent with biblical relationships. If your leadership group struggles with unhealthy relationships and practices at the leadership level, none of the principles of this book will help until this issue is resolved.

Once a board has agreed to live by relational, biblical principles and its members are holding one another accountable, they can go to the congregation and ask that the congregation as a whole live by those principles. This is a powerful teaching tool and a powerful way to change what may have been poor relational practices within the church. Congregations are usually willing to follow their leaders.

COVENANT OF HEALTHY RELATIONSHIPS

Knowing that we, as leaders of this congregation, must model godly relationships before one another and the church, we commit ourselves to:

- Pray daily for fellow members of the leadership team and for the ministry of the church
- Never speak ill of any member of the team
- Resolve broken relationships personally and quickly
- Forgive one another when offended and hold no grudges
- Always support decisions of this board once they are made, unless a biblical, moral issue is at stake
- Care for one another when a member is hurting
- Always be honest in board deliberations and never devious in seeking personal agendas
- Never betray a confidence of the board
- Hold one another accountable for this covenant and agree to step off the board if there is regular violation of these agreements

CAN THE FUNDAMENTAL GENETIC CODE OF A CONGREGATION CHANGE?

When leaders are committed to healthy relationships and DNA, they often wonder if the fundamental genetic code of a congregation can really change. This is really a question of whether a congregation with a troubled history and a great deal of unhealthy genetic code can see substantial spiritual renovation. In my experience, the answer is yes—if church leaders understand the issues at hand, take a long-term view of congregational renovation, and resolutely trust God. Such spiritual renovation is most likely achieved if it is recognized as a process and if leaders are willing to pay the personal cost to guide the congregation into spiritual health. If in reading this chapter you realize that significant renovation is necessary in your congregation, I encourage you to believe that God wants exactly that for your church and that He is even more desirous of change than you are.

One of the keys to transformation is the leaders' willingness to set the standard and commit themselves to healthy practices. Congregations are much more likely to respond when leaders set the pace. This is why healthy and unified leadership boards are far more likely to grow congregations that are healthy and unified. When unhealthy practices are identified, church leaders should first look honestly at themselves and ask where they have either contributed to or engaged in unhealthy practices.

In the case of one of the congregations I was part of, both the congregation and the board had contributed to unhealthy practices—but when the leaders committed to change, they were able to lead the congregation in it as well.

LEADING CHANGE

In this church, we had a long-standing history of dealing with conflict by talking to everyone except the individual with whom we had a problem. Clearly, this had to be dealt with, but it was not going to change overnight. The tendency was rooted in our culture, which did not like to "confront" those who had offended us, but ended up making issues worse by talking to others instead. Not only was that bad practice, it also violated basic biblical principles.

When we realized this, we saw that the board had indirectly contributed to the problem by allowing people to bring complaints to us rather than sending them back to the one against whom they had a complaint. We were violating Matthew 18 principles and unintentionally allowing unhealthy practices to perpetuate themselves. In solving the problem, we had to change our practices before asking the congregation to change theirs. Leaders change first!

Then we decided to address the issue with the congregation in three ways.

First, we talked and taught about the problem. We addressed it from the pulpit and in our discipleship classes. We taught God's expectations for conflict resolution and the steps we would follow in the congregation.

Second, leaders resolved that whenever someone brought them a complaint about someone else, we would ask, "Have you talked with the person you are unhappy with?" If the answer was no, we would tell them we weren't willing to discuss the issue until they had talked to those with whom they had an offense. If the answer was yes, and there still was not resolution, we would go with them to seek resolution. We also openly shared our policy with the congregation.

Third, we affirmed those who followed the biblical model privately and, where appropriate, publicly. Those who followed the steps found it worked — and generated far less stress and conflict. Members even began encouraging one another to deal with these issues in a God-honoring manner rather than through gossip or third-party conversations.

This part of our unhealthy culture substantially changed — but not overnight. It took two years. Churches change slowly. They are made up of people who, as a rule, do not find change easy! (Before we become impatient with those we lead, we need to remember how long it takes us to deal with issues in our lives.)

While most change happens slowly, there are some instances when leaders must deal with negative practices by talking truthfully, forthrightly, and directly with their congregation. Examples of these times include a significant moral issue or a conflict that threatens to divide the body. This intervention is most likely to succeed if the pastor and leaders are in complete agreement (and this is known to the congregation), if the message has been bathed in prayer beforehand, and if leaders understand the ramifications of what they are doing and have counted the cost. It is also crucial that leaders have done everything they can to resolve the issue before taking it to the congregation as a whole.

CONGREGATIONS CAN SEE RENOVATION

Renovation of a congregation is a process that requires God's power, wise and courageous leaders, and great patience. Before we look at the steps toward renovation, I want to complete the story of Faith Church. Something powerful emerged from the vision process, coupled with the resulting conflict that led to the exodus of a core group: leaders who were committed to understand the congregation's genetic code, face unpleasant realities, and chart a new course. The process of renovation took a number of years, and it was not easy for the leaders or the congregation. However, those who stuck it through (all the leadership did) look back in amazement at what God did.

The way disagreements were handled during that conflict caused the board to look at Faith's history of periodic conflict. They realized that all too often conflict went unresolved or was resolved poorly. This included a pastor who had left the church feeling deeply wounded.

They also realized that Faith, from its founding, had a history of mistrusting its leadership. This mistrust continued to manifest itself whenever leaders started to give direction. An outside facilitator was invited to help walk them through a process of confession and of setting new direction for dealing with one another.

Faith also realized it was still doing leadership as it had when it was a small church of one hundred, even after having grown to almost five hundred. Leaders determined they needed to *lead* or the church's growth would plateau. This led to discussions with the congregation as to what leadership looked like in a larger church versus a small "family" church.

The conflict also revealed multiple visions of what Faith should be. Leaders had not clarified their philosophy of ministry or direction over the years, afraid the ensuing discussion would lead to disagreement. The result was that different groups assumed differing visions, eventually leading to greater conflict than was necessary. It was clear that Faith had to decide who it would be and what direction it would take. Building on the work of the vision committee, the leadership and pastoral staff members continued to clarify Faith's focus and build into the church a set of values, mission, and vision for the future. All of this was done with the involvement of the congregation.

The vision process had raised a spiritual issue of how dependent the leadership and congregation were on God's power for their ministry. They were deeply convicted that Faith had a history of spiritual pride and a low level of spiritual dependence. The leadership confessed this to the congregation—not an easy thing to do—and together, they started to pray more, both corporately and personally. They knew the crisis had revealed spiritual fault lines that, unless acknowledged and dealt with, would block Faith from the kind of ministry impact many were longing for.

These decisions, directions, new ways of dealing with one another, and dependence on God were reinforced in small groups, from the pulpit, and in discipleship classes. At every level, individuals and groups were encouraged to pray for the church and its future. Because these were spiritual issues as well as leadership and cultural issues, only the Holy Spirit could ultimately lead to spiritual and lasting renovation.

This was often a painful time for leaders. Even after the group of dissidents departed, questions and malicious, untrue gossip about leaders remained (and spread to other churches in town). This was especially painful for leaders who were giving their lives to see Faith move into a bright ministry future.

As is often the case in churches undergoing spiritual renovation, attrition continued for various reasons. Some people were weary of conflict, some impatient for the new vision to take root, some unhappy with the new vision, and others unhappy with leadership. Each time another left, the leaders felt as if a raw wound was being reopened.

Then one day, something significant happened. People noticed that congregational meetings were no longer contentious. Relationships were healthier. The sniping and gossip had disappeared. There was excitement about the future and, for the first time (according to long-time members), a common vision. Significant spiritual renovation had taken root. It felt like a different church—and it was! Much of the negative genetic code had been discarded for a new and healthier one. Some called it a church *restart*. Faith continues to this day with a vibrant spiritual climate of expectancy. Now, people are no longer leaving; they're coming—and staying. It is a new church.

STEPS TO RENOVATION

Few outcomes are more satisfying for a church leader than to see a congregation that has been sick and unhealthy emerge from renovation vibrant, healthy, and energized for God's work. Here are some steps to remember and expect as you walk through the process.

Remind yourself that crisis can be a friend. As it does in individuals, spiritual renovation for congregations often starts in crisis. The pain is an ally for those who will listen—a wake-up call that not all is well. Rather than run, wise leaders use a crisis to ask important questions about health, the past, and the future. Crises reveal spiritual fault lines in a congregation that need to be addressed. Left unaddressed, they become wider and deeper.

Start to lead more intentionally. A congregation will not move from an unhealthy state to a healthy one without significant leadership. In fact, as the leaders at Faith saw, many of the issues uncovered in their crisis were a result of poor board leadership over the years. Spiritual renovation of a congregation requires courageous leaders who are not afraid to face brutal facts, who are willing to admit sin and make commitments to change, and who will lead their congregation in a healthy spiritual direction.

Face reality. "Walk toward the barking dog" is one of my favorite mottos. Wise leaders face reality rather than run from it, no matter how painful or unpleasant. Walking toward that dog is a necessary prerequisite to healing and wholeness.

The leaders at Faith took a long, hard look at the spiritual climate of their church, past and present. The more they looked, the more they didn't like what they saw. Poor interpersonal relationships, spiritual pride, and lack of direction are not pleasant realities to admit. However, the clearer a leadership board can be about negative issues, the more effectively it can tackle root causes.

Leaders in troubled congregations must clearly understand the issues that have contributed to their current condition. This will take prayer, discussion, thought, and often the help of an outside facilitator. Not everything you discover must be made public, but as leaders you need understanding.

Confess sinful practices. Significant areas of sin (often the root of unhealthy genetics) need to be confessed and renounced by church leaders. While this is difficult, remember how often confession was the precursor to renewal in the Old Testament. God embraces those who confess.

The naming of the sin along with its confession is a powerful step for church leaders. Like Daniel (see Daniel 9), you may be confessing your own sin or the sins of your predecessors. Consider asking a wise outside facilitator to help you walk through this process.

Covenant to new practices. Unhealthy and sinful practices need to be replaced by healthy and godly practices. This new genetic code needs to be specified and articulated. A written document can become a reminder of your commitment to renovation — one that articulates both what has been confessed and what new practices have been embraced.

After the leadership has committed to it, consider sharing the confession and commitments with your congregation and invite them to walk with you in healthy and godly practices. Don't be surprised if you encounter some resistance. Not everyone is going to be as excited as you because not all will want to admit they have been part of the problem.

Ingrained habits are not easily changed.

Recruit a guiding coalition. Significant change across a congregation takes more than the influence of the leadership board. Bring other church leaders into the process who can embrace and model the changes with you. Invite them to sign the same covenant and agree to the same commitments. Talk about how the larger leadership community can support the change process and influence their circle of contacts to make the same commitments. When a church's whole leadership community agrees to new ways of relating or ministering, it makes a powerful statement to the congregation at large and starts to create "cascades" of support.

Model, teach, and establish new practices. At this point, you will need to be proactive in teaching, modeling, and establishing new godly practices at every level of ministry. Talk frankly from the pulpit, in small- and large-group settings, in membership classes—wherever you can—to remind the congregation of who you are and your commitments to be the authentic body of Jesus Christ. At all costs, keep the issues in front of the leadership community so you can model that to which you have called the congregation.

Establish a prayer coalition. Things happen when people pray. The Holy Spirit starts to remind us of positive behaviors and convict us of sinful behaviors. Encourage a new humility before God, being honest with Him about the issues you face and claiming His promises for renewal when His people humble themselves before Him (see 2 Chronicles 7:14).

Engage a prayer team to ask God to bring change to the congregation. Encourage your leadership community to pray daily about these issues. Use congregational and small-group opportunities to pray for renewal. See the prayer strategy as a long-term commitment.

Don't be surprised if the situation gets worse before it gets better. I often warn couples who go for marital counseling that things will get worse before they get better. A counselor is going to unearth painful history that has been stuffed over the years on the way to getting at the dysfunction in the marriage. Once those issues are out in the open, the wound can be dealt with, but the process leading to a renewed marriage can be painful.

The same is true in a congregation. Remember the pain Faith experienced as it walked through renovation? If your church commits to the same process, at times you will look at one another and ask, "What have we gotten ourselves into?" You may well feel wounded and abused and deeply discouraged in the process. But just like I tell married couples, expect the downturn and hang in there

Realize that it's okay when people leave during renovation. If you have walked with church leadership through significant crisis and change, you know how discouraging it is to come to meeting after meeting and hear the latest list of those who have left the church. But you should expect people to leave during the renovation; it's okay that it happens.

When I write that it's okay, I'm not necessarily saying I want it to happen. However, it does, and sometimes it is for the best. Consider:

- By the time people decide to leave, there is usually nothing you can do or say to keep them — they have already left emotionally.
- Spiritual renovation will leave some people cold — people who have no desire or intention of renovating their attitudes or changing their behavior. This is part of living in a sinful world, and we cannot force them to change.
- When leaders start to lead well, they help the congregation clarify who they are and what their future is. Clarification causes some to say, "I don't want to be on this bus anymore. It's going in a direction I don't want to go." Not only is that a legitimate decision, but they will not be happy passengers if they don't want to be on your bus. Far better they find a church where they can minister with a happy heart and a good conscience than stay in yours with an unhappy heart and a bad attitude.
- People leave even when leaders are holding to the status quo. Sometimes this happens because people sense the church is unhealthy and leaders are fearful of confronting change, so the very people you need in order to become a healthy church end

up leaving to find one. The question is not *whether* people will leave, but *which* people will leave.

- People often take up the offenses of others. Thus, when an individual is disgruntled and decides to leave, it is not unusual for his or her friends to do the same, even when they are not personally affected and do not know all the facts.

- Finally, healthy churches have a significant amount of philosophical unity. The congregation agrees on who they are and where they are going. Part of becoming healthy is agreeing on fundamentals such as values the congregation will live by and the future they will embrace. Those who disagree either need to change or find a congregation consistent with their convictions.

Hang in there, trust God, keep praying, and lead wisely. Spiritual renovation is not easy and rarely fast. However, God wants to bring renewal. If leaders are patient, stay the course, do what is right, and keep praying, chances are good that renovation will come. Both for purposes of wisdom and encouragement, I recommend you find an outside cheerleader and coach, perhaps a leader from another church who has walked through a successful change process. Many of the dynamics of congregational renovation are similar, so such an individual can provide encouragement and perspective when the days seem long.

HOW HEALTHY IS YOUR CONGREGATION?

No doubt, this chapter has caused you to think about the health of your congregation. If this is the case, I am pleased, because becoming and remaining healthy are the ongoing concerns of good leaders. Simply put, healthy congregations represent Christ best. They are also best able to build healthy disciples and to engage in healthy ministry.

Alternatively, unhealthy congregations hurt people, hurt the reputation of Christ, and keep His followers from meaningful ministry to a hurting world. If your congregation is unhealthy, don't run. Face reality and proactively work toward spiritual renovation.

H. I. MOMENT

In what ways is our congregation healthy?

Are there any significant areas of illness? Where did these come from?

Which issues must we as leaders help the congregation deal with to become a healthier congregation?

H. I. WRAP-UP: STEPS TO CONGREGATIONAL RENOVATION

- Remind yourself that crisis can be a friend.
- Start to lead intentionally.
- Face reality.
- Confess sinful practices.
- Covenant to new practices.
- Recruit a guiding coalition.
- Model, teach, and establish new practices.
- Establish a prayer coalition.
- Don't be surprised if the situation gets worse before it gets better.
- Realize that it's okay when people leave during renovation.
- Hang in there, trust God, keep praying, and lead wisely.

Part Two

INTENTIONAL LEADERS

If you always do what you always did,

you always get what you always got.

— POSTER

And for the church of Jesus, that is unacceptable.

Chapter Six

A PARABLE OF TWO HOUSES

Once a private home in the community of San Jose, California, the Winchester House is now a major tourist attraction — not for its beauty or usefulness, but rather for its story and unique lack of functionality!

The home was built by Sarah Winchester, the widow of William Winchester, one of the owners of Winchester Rifles. Sarah had been previously devastated by the loss of a baby and suffered under the delusion that she, too, would die unless her home remained under construction. Thus, for the next twenty years, she kept carpenters and builders on the job twenty-four hours a day pounding nails, sawing boards, squaring walls, laying brick, and glazing windows.

What makes this unique home a tourist attraction is Sarah's total lack of a master plan — all that mattered to her was that the activity continue. The result is a well-built and expensive architectural chaos. The 24,000 square feet contains 160 rooms, 40 staircases, 5 or 6 kitchens, and 47 fireplaces. Visitors are in for a surprise at every turn. Staircases ascend into the ceiling — literally. Doors open onto brick walls or even open spaces with a several-story drop! Corridors lead nowhere, and windows show only wallboards. Remarkable in its quintessential uniqueness, it draws thousands of visitors each year from around the world.

Another home sits on the cliffs above the Mississippi River in rural Wisconsin. Appropriately named Prairie Ledge, it belongs to my friends Grant and Carol, and is a picture of beauty, strength, long planning, and tasteful decorating — all of it finished with remarkable craftsmanship. From this craggy setting, guests can see the mighty river below, eagles soaring overhead, and a far horizon in three directions. Wild turkeys, grouse, foxes, rabbits, squirrels, and deer inhabit the property.

Unlike the Winchester house, Prairie Ledge was conceived and built with minute attention to detail in order to achieve specific ends. Starting with several nonnegotiables, an architect spent more than a year designing this spectacular but functional home, followed by another year of building. The end result brings joy not only to Grant and Carol but also to the hundreds of friends they invite to enjoy Prairie Ledge each year.

SOMETHING TO THINK ABOUT

If you were building a home, which of these models would you follow? Probably not one of us would follow Sarah's lead. We wouldn't enter into the expensive, time-consuming, and important task of building a house without the most well-conceived and functional plan we could afford. A poorly conceived or poorly built home costs us for years down the road—in stress, money, functionality, and energy.

As you go about the leadership job of planning, designing, and implementing ministry, are you following the model of the Winchester House or Prairie Ledge?

I have shared this illustration with numerous church boards, and all too often I receive nods of acknowledgment that, yes, we are building ministry by the Winchester model. Over the years, we pile program on top of program, ministry upon ministry (each of them "looking good" when started), until alignment, coherence, or direction is difficult to discern.

The Winchester House illustrates what I call "accidental ministry." Ministry is more random than planned, usually without a coherent philosophy or clear picture of what we desire it to look like in the future. This doesn't mean these ministries are fruitless; good things can happen "accidentally"—for which we thank God.

Prairie Ledge is a metaphor for intentional ministry. The house was conceived as a dream, but the dream was then systematically translated into reality through planning and careful execution. Healthy churches and healthy leadership practices, as described in part 1 of this book, never happen accidentally. They are the result of intentional ministry where the power of God's Spirit and the best of God's leaders are brought to bear on the mission Christ left for His church.

Ironically, we would never use the accidental or Winchester approach when we build our actual church facilities. All too often, however, we allow the accidental approach to characterize what is far more important than our physical structures: the ministries of our churches! This leads to unforeseen consequences.

In their 2001 book, *Lost in America*, authors Tom Clegg and Warren Bird shared what they call "seven deadly statistics" about the spiritual status of our nation—all of which are, sadly, still true today:

> *Fact 1*: The percentage of adults in the United States who attend church is decreasing.
>
> *Fact 2:* Roughly half of all churches in America did not add one new person through conversion last year.
>
> *Fact 3*: No matter how you do the math, current conversion rules still point to one horrible conclusion: Lost people lose.
>
> *Fact 4*: Some researchers claim more churches are closing than are opening each year.
>
> *Fact 5*: Conversions to other religions and dropouts from Christianity are escalating.
>
> *Fact 6*: The decline in Christianity has been going on for nearly fifty years.
>
> *Fact 7*: Too many churched people believe and behave identically to their unchurched counterparts.[1]

Regardless of who does the research, the findings are the same: These are challenging days for the church. Christ called us to introduce the world to Him, yet in America it takes "the combined efforts of 85 Christians working over an entire year to produce one convert."[2] The church has been tasked to help people grow into fully devoted Christ followers, yet there seems to be little difference between the behavior and commitments of believers compared with nonbelievers.[3]

KEY QUESTIONS FOR CHURCH LEADERS

In the face of this, the first question we are forced to ask is, "How can it be that we see such anemic ministry results in the most churched nation in our world?" It is my conviction that the answer is directly related to the ability or inability of leaders to clarify four critical leadership concerns:

1. *Who are we?* What are our nonnegotiables? What are our guiding values — those things that are unchanging about our ministry and that must guide everything we do?
2. *Why do we exist?* Why are we here? What is the mission of our church? What is the driving purpose to which we give ourselves?
3. *Where are we going?* What is our preferred future? What is our vision for where we desire to go? Can we describe the kind of ministry we are building?
4. *How will we get there?* What do we need to do now? What do we do next? What truly strategic issues must we tackle so that we get where we desire to go? Do we have a plan for building our ministry?

Church leaders routinely flock to churches such as Saddleback, Willow Creek, and North Coast, hungry for strategies and programs. Yet too often they forget that even deeper than any strategy — be it seeker services, baseball diamonds, or video cafés — lies the reality that these successful ministries are flourishing not primarily because of specific strategies (good as the strategies are). Rather, they are relying on God's Spirit and His power as they simultaneously answer these four leadership questions and develop their ministries with intentionality.

These ministries know their nonnegotiables. They have clarified their mission. They have formed a compelling picture of their preferred future and are working an intentional plan to get there. They have chosen to do ministry strategically rather than randomly. They yearn for God's power and the best wisdom at the same time.

The juxtaposition of God's call on the church and the meager ministry results of many churches begs another question every church-leadership group must struggle with: "What will we settle for in our ministry?" The fact that you are reading this book is an indication you are not satisfied with where your church is. I would guess you long for more of God's power, for deeper spiritual change in the lives of your people, and for your congregation to make a deeper impact on your community and the world. Jesus also longs for your church to have that impact.

The parable of the talents in Matthew 25 is usually applied on an individual basis. But is it not also appropriate to apply it corporately? In the parable, the Father praised those who had multiplied ministry for Him — who were strategic in how they used what He had given them. At the same time, He condemned the one who buried his talents, too frightened to put them into play. Similarly, just as Jesus either applauded or chastised the seven churches of Revelation for their corporate love and ministry on His behalf, does it not also follow that He will either be pleased or disappointed with the leadership we have performed on His behalf?

Because so many churches have settled for unintentional or accidental ministry, we have the situation described by the authors of *Lost in America*. But it need not be that way. And for a growing number of congregations, it is not that way. Those who are deeply intentional are seeing lasting spiritual fruit.

Great ministry does not happen by accident. Church health is not a random condition. It is a result of a disciplined commitment to become everything we can be with the resources God has given us. To be great is to embrace the same commitment to mission-driven ministry that Jesus modeled for us.

JESUS AND MISSION-DRIVEN MINISTRY

Jesus said to His Father in His prayer in John 17, "I have brought you glory on earth by completing the work you gave me to do" (verse 4).

That mission is no better described than in John 3:16: "For God so loved the world that he gave his one and only Son, that whoever believes in him shall not perish but have eternal life."

Jesus was quick to reject the advice of His closest disciples when they suggested that He violate or modify His mission. In fulfillment of that mission, Jesus ate with sinners, talked to and loved those who were unclean, wooed or condemned Pharisees, continued to train His disciples even when they failed, and went to Jerusalem knowing death awaited. Jesus did whatever it took to fulfill His mission, whether or not it violated social norms. The only nonnegotiables were the mission He pursued and the principles He adhered to.

Jesus lived by nonnegotiables. As I read the Gospels, five of Jesus' nonnegotiables or guiding principles (values) leap out at me.

- Dependence on the Father
- Obedience to the Father
- Adherence to the Word
- Loving people into His kingdom
- Glorifying the Father

Jesus enjoyed poking fun at the status quo: challenging the assumptions of the Pharisees and of His own disciples, hanging with people classified as sinners, and teaching a radical way of thinking about God. The one thing Jesus never did, however, was violate the set of values by which He lived. After His divinity, these values were what defined who He was and how He lived.

H. I. BEST PRACTICE

Never violate your nonnegotiables — but make sure you have the right nonnegotiables!

Jesus carried a vision for the future. Jesus lived with a clear and compelling picture of the future: a vibrant, effective, flexible, passionate, dependent, obedient, fruitful church committed to loving God and reaching every culture in every generation. I am sure that vision encouraged Him when He was tempted to become disheartened. Pieces of that vision spill out all over the place in the Gospels.

It was a vision that allowed Jesus to choose disciples to establish the church whom others would consider second-string players. Jesus could put up with their issues, failures, and foibles because He had faith in what they could be and what they would become. This picture—a vibrant church led by leaders passionate for Him and His flock—informed His training, teaching, and an optimistic attitude in the face of insurmountable odds.

Often, Jesus connected what He and the disciples were doing with His larger vision. For instance, in Matthew 9, the disciples were overwhelmed by the needs of the diseased and sick crowds. Jesus didn't see crowds but individuals who were "harassed and helpless, like sheep without a shepherd" and urged the disciples to "ask the Lord . . . to send out workers into his harvest field" (verses 36,38). He envisioned a day when they—and we—would have the same vision for needy crowds.

In the Sermon on the Mount, Jesus gave His disciples a picture of what life in His kingdom looks like. Then, in His parting words of the Great Commission, Jesus conveyed His dream: a multiplying band of disciples who are helping people find His grace and grow into spiritual maturity. Jesus pictured a future full of opportunity, spiritual growth, church expansion, revolutionized lives, and spiritual influence.

It was this picture of God's future that drove Jesus to the cross, knowing its pain and abandon. After His resurrection and ascension, this picture of a grace-filled future drove the disciples to give their lives, literally and figuratively, for Jesus' kingdom.

Jesus ministered intentionally. Jesus was deeply purposeful in how He pursued His mission and His picture of the preferred future. Before choosing His disciples, He spent a long time in prayer. Rather than ministering to the devoted crowds, Jesus took time to train twelve men, along with a wider circle of seventy-two others. Before He sent them out on their own, they lived and ministered with Him, observing Him. Piece by piece He taught them about Himself, His Father, His kingdom, and the future.

The Gospels portray a Savior who lived with intentionality and balance. They depict a ministry that is strategic, bathed in prayer, wise in timing and teaching, and committed to long-term results. We are heirs of this mission, and Jesus is calling us to the same kind of value-laden, mission-driven, future-focused, and strategically driven ministry.

STRATEGIC, INTENTIONAL MINISTRY

Part 2 will demonstrate how healthy leaders engage in intentional ministry through an understanding of values, mission, preferred future, and ministry initiatives.

This is not about strategic planning. It is about doing ministry intentionally so that we maximize the opportunities Christ has given our congregations and thus multiply kingdom ministry.

It is about being proactive rather than reactive, strategic rather than random, with a bias toward action rather than feeling comfortable with the status quo. Intentional ministry is possible no matter what size your congregation. It is strategic ministry that allows us to multiply the kingdom potential of our congregations.

H. I. MOMENT

Are the ministries of our church more accidental or intentional? What evidence leads me to this conclusion?

Does our leadership team have clear answers to the four fundamental questions every organization must be able to answer? Is there agreement among our key staff members and leaders about our answers?

H. I. WRAP-UP: QUESTIONS FOR HIGH-IMPACT LEADERS

- Who are we? What are our nonnegotiables?
- Why do we exist? Why are we here?
- Where are we going? What is our preferred future?
- How will we get there? What do we need to do now?

Chapter Seven

VALUES: DETERMINING THE NONNEGOTIABLES

I've spent some of my most enjoyable days with my buddy Mark on his yacht off Gulf Shores, Alabama. As we cruise the inland waterway toward the open gulf for a day of deep-sea fishing, we have one priority: Stay between the red and green buoys!

If we were to stray outside the channel marked by the buoys, the bottom of the boat would be in for an expensive surprise—as many others have learned. The channel is safe, but the rest of the wide waterway is not. The buoys are guides designed to keep us inside the safe channel.

This is the purpose of godly values: They are guides that keep us within the channel where God wants us. Values are the nonnegotiable guiding principles by which an organization is committed to live.

Properly understood, prayerfully determined, and carefully defined, values are powerful tools that help mold us personally and organizationally into what we desire to become. When values are cherished and lived out, they facilitate change and guard against the drift that would take us away from the best to the merely good . . . or even to the sinful and destructive.

In the gulf you can inadvertently leave the channel if you are not constantly vigilant. On many parts of the inland waterway, the wise pilot always eyes the buoys; it's second nature. Once you learn to live by values and trust them to keep you in God's channel for your life or ministry, they become second nature, too. Whether personal or organizational, the nonnegotiable principles around which we organize our lives and ministries help us stay true to what God has called us to be.

VALUES ARE ORGANIZING PRINCIPLES

Jesus carefully defined His nonnegotiables and organized His life around them. In doing so, He stayed true to a life of intimacy, obedience, and dependence upon His Father. Without well-defined values, we are less likely to organize our ministries in ways consistent with God's call. This is not because we care don't care about His call but because we have not defined what is "core" about it and thus risk drifting from it, allowing the less important and even the trivial to define our churches.

In the denominational office where I work, we have identified four core values to support our mission of serving churches and constituents.

1. *Leadership: We take responsibility.* We take responsibility for performing our duties with excellence and for initiating ways to improve the service we provide.
2. *Integrity: We are above reproach.* We are committed to honest practices, communication, and relationships that honor Jesus Christ and one another.
3. *Learning: We are committed to growth.* We view learning as an ongoing process and seek opportunities to improve ourselves both personally and professionally.
4. *Teamwork: We work together.* We practice mutual cooperation and communication both within and outside of our departments in order to accomplish our common mission.

These are the nonnegotiable guiding principles around which each of the hundred or so employees—from the president to the front-desk operator—organizes his or her work. If a call comes to my office that should have been directed elsewhere, the *leadership* value of "taking responsibility" means I must either personally ensure the caller is connected with the right person or find an answer to the question and return the call. Where cooperation is required, I have no choice but to work with others because of the *teamwork* value of working together.

To ensure everyone understands these shared values, every job description lists the responsibility to uphold and live by them. Our annual reviews include an evaluation of our adherence to our values, and each year, all employees indicate how they are going to uphold the mission and values in the coming year. Their statements go to the president for his review and personal signature.

H. I. MOMENT

What are the four highest values for our church? (Ask board members to share their four, creating a list that can be refined later.)

1. _____

2. _____

3. _____

4. _____

VALUES BRING ALIGNMENT

In our office, the values have become the buoys between which each team member operates. These values have had another significant effect: Because we are all committed to them, we experience a high level of alignment. Everyone is enthusiastic about serving our churches and constituents.

When values are inculcated at every level of an organization, you will find divine creativity flowing out of those who live by those values. For example, many visitors are surprised when Mel, who staffs our front desk, prays for their needs. "Wow," they say, "I can't believe that guy." Mel is uniquely exercising the leadership value of taking responsibility for their needs. Can you imagine the impact of a whole congregation living out a set of biblical values through the power of the Holy Spirit?

VALUES RULE OUT CERTAIN OPTIONS

When my friends Grant and Carol built Prairie Ledge, they searched for an architect who could help them bring their dreams to reality. They gave him several nonnegotiable principles that would guide his work, including the guideline that construction materials needed to fit the natural resources of the area. That value left many options open to him but closed others. For instance, he could use Wisconsin limestone on the facade but not New England marble.

Likewise, an organization's values leave many options open but rule others out. This can be very helpful when people are deciding whether they want to become part of our ministries. As part of the hiring process at our office, we make our values crystal clear to the individual under consideration. If the person agrees with them and wants to join us, we do multiple reference checks to gauge the honesty of that statement. Bringing on board staff members who are not in concert with our values is not an option, no matter how professionally competent they are.

We can also make the nonnegotiables clear on the front end with people who are considering joining our churches, which allows them to decide if the congregation is a good fit—our nonnegotiables are not going to change. So if a new attendee brings with him values that are "anti-values" for you, as often happens when someone is coming from another congregation, you are upfront that this is not who you are.

A best practice I have seen in growing churches is when the senior pastor periodically invites new attendees to a dessert at his home. During this time, the pastor welcomes attendees and describes who the church is and who the church is not. By making clear on the front end what they hold dear, church leaders guard the channels of their congregations.

VALUES WILL BE UNIQUE

Because every congregation is different, the values they cherish will be unique as well. This is why it is imperative not to adopt another congregation's values. Your congregation will not be committed to them, no matter how good they may sound. Well-chosen values reflect the uniqueness of a congregation and the nonnegotiables for its ministry.

Following are the values for two unique congregations. As you examine them, try to identify the core guiding principles around which each one crafts its ministries.

Two Rivers Church
Knoxville, Tennessee

Our core values are to live . . .

> . . . beyond rituals of religious ceremony to enjoying God in public worship and private devotion.
> . . . beyond theory about God to experiencing life-changing biblical truth in the context of meaningful relationships.
> . . . beyond relational isolation to connecting our lives together in genuine Christian community.
> . . . beyond spectator Christianity to embracing our unique and essential role as God directs us in joining the expansion of His kingdom.
> . . . beyond evangelical and charismatic extremes to embracing the best of both.
> . . . beyond self-centeredness to caring for those in need.
> . . . beyond fear of telling others about Jesus to enthusiastically telling others our personal story.
> . . . beyond growing our church only to starting churches in other communities.[1]

Heartland Community Church
Rockford, Illinois

> **Value 1:** We believe that anointed teaching is the catalyst for transformation in individuals' lives and in the church. This includes the concept of teaching for life change. (Romans 12:7; 2 Timothy 3:16-17; James 1:23-25)

Value 2: We believe that lost people matter to God, and therefore, they matter to us. This includes the concepts of relational evangelism and evangelism as a process. (Matthew 18:14; Luke 5:30-32; Luke 15)

Value 3: We believe that the church should be culturally relevant while remaining doctrinally pure. This includes the concepts of sensitively relating the gospel to our culture through our facility, printed materials, and the use of technology, media, and the arts. (1 Corinthians 9:19-23)

Value 4: We believe that life change happens best in the authentic community of a small group of people. This includes the concepts of discipleship, vulnerability, and accountability. (Luke 6:12-13; Acts 2:44-47)

Value 5: We believe that excellence honors God and inspires people. This includes the concepts of evaluation, critical review, intensity, and excellence. (Proverbs 27:17; Malachi 1:6-14; Colossians 3:17)

Value 6: We believe the church and its ministries should be led by men and women with the spiritual gift of leadership. This includes the concepts of empowerment, servant leadership, strategic focus, and intentionality. (Nehemiah 1–2; Acts 6:2-5; Romans 12:8)

Value 7: We believe that the pursuit of full devotion to Christ and His cause is normal for every believer. This includes the concepts of stewardship, servanthood, downward mobility, and the pursuit of kingdom goals. (1 Kings 11:4; 2 Corinthians 8:7; Philippians 2:1-11)

Value 8: We believe that people need to have space in their lives to engage in life. This includes the concepts of appropriate work/rest cycle, family life, and relational evangelism. (Genesis 2:2; Proverbs 23:4; Matthew 5:29-32)

Value 9: We believe that a submitted life aligned with one's spiritual gifts is the way God leverages us as individuals and as a church for His kingdom. This includes the concepts of listening to God, saying "yes" to God, using spiritual gifts, and serving others. (Matthew 4:18-22; Ephesians 4:11-12; 1 Peter 4:10)

Value 10: We believe that unity in the church is essential. This includes the concepts of conflict resolution, believing the best in each other, not allowing conflict to go underground, speaking well of others, and not listening to or participating in gossip. (Psalm 133:1; Matthew 18:15-17; Ephesians 4:2–6:16)[2]

VALUES HELP CHURCHES LIVE INTENTIONALLY

Values help organizations live intentionally rather than randomly. I chose these two churches to illustrate values because in each case the leadership has done the hard work of determining the guiding principles by which they will live. These nonnegotiables describe the cultures they are building and become the grid against which all ministries and decisions are evaluated.

Two Rivers Church has consistently been generous with hurting and needy people. We have already seen that they committed to give away 10 percent of what they raised for a new building to other ministries. This is consistent with their value of living "beyond self-centeredness to caring for those in need." Under its value of being "outreach-oriented," Wooddale Church in Eden Prairie, Minnesota, says that "when a choice is made between serving needs on the inside or reaching out to others, we are committed in advance toward ministry to outsiders."[3] This value keeps ministry within the channel of outreach.

In these churches, the values have molded the people, culture, and ministries to a significant degree. The values represent the channel within which the life and ministries of these congregations flow. When water flows out of the channel, it means a value has been violated, and leaders can quickly act to bring the ministry flow back within the value's guides.

Without clearly and carefully defined values, we do not have the needed channel markers to minister intentionally rather than randomly. Seen in this light, values help us make critical decisions in a realm where there are always many options and decisions bring consequences.

VALUES DEFINE A CHURCH'S PREFERRED CULTURE

Two Rivers Church and Heartland Community Church use their values to define their preferred culture. These churches value a kingdom mind-set. They value authentic relationships, deep Christianity, genuine concern for the lost and the disadvantaged, and strong commitments to the Word of God. Church cultures that reflect values such as these are attractive, accepting, open, inviting, grace-filled, and friendly. All of us have visited churches where this has not been the case.

Because the natural tendency of organizations over time is to focus inwardly ("We exist for the people already here") rather than outwardly ("We exist for those who are not yet with us"), it is easy for church cultures to feel friendly for those on the inside but unfriendly from the outside. Undefined and unguarded cultures are therefore dangerous for the church whose very mission is to reach those who do not know Christ and to help them become whole persons within the context of a healthy community.

Congregations who have defined their preferred culture and who use biblical values to help foster and guard that culture have opportunities to fulfill the Great Commission that other congregations do not have. Defining your preferred culture through carefully thought-out values is a key factor in building healthy, intentional ministries.

THE PROCESS OF DETERMINING VALUES

One of the reasons it is helpful for churches to identify their values is that every person and every church has a set, whether written or unwritten.

We have been talking up to now about values that reflect God's call on our ministries. Yet the values we hold can be positive or negative.

The individual who values positional advancement over family has a core value, but it is a destructive one. To clarify your church's character, think about positive values that are already ingrained in your congregation. These might include embodying grace and eschewing legalism, creating a welcoming environment for those struggling with addictions, or strengthening families and marriages.

H. I. MOMENT

What are the top five positive characteristics of our congregation?

1. _____
2. _____
3. _____
4. _____
5. _____

Equally important is the need to identify values that may be problematic (recall chapter 5 on church DNA). These are often nonnegotiables by which the congregation lives, though they are unspoken.

Your current values (written or unwritten) may or may not reflect those you wish to characterize your congregation. Leaders need to ask, "What do we believe God wants us to look like? What values or organizing principles do we believe He wants for us, and to which values are we willing to make hard and fast commitments?" The question is not simply *Who are we?* but *Who do we believe God wants us to be?*

If your church has not already determined your values, here are some questions that can help:

- What do we understand God's nonnegotiable priorities for a church to be?
- What are our highest unchanging priorities?
- How do we want our church to be known?

- What will distinguish our congregation from others?
- If we had to describe to a visitor the five to eight key truths or commitments by which we live, what would they be?
- What is our preferred culture for our congregation?

As you begin to compile your values list, remember that values should not be confused with methods or strategies, which define how a congregation will live out its nonnegotiables. Nor are they a statement of faith, although an evangelical church would undoubtedly define its commitment to God's Word as one of its nonnegotiables.

Whether you state your values in full sentences or pithy phrases, include an explanation of each one so members and visitors understand the channel markers of the church.

How many core values should you have? I generally recommend fewer than ten. The desire to include *everything* in your values will decrease their effectiveness. Values will only be helpful if people live them; when you have many, it is difficult for people to make them their own. If you can get the number down to five, you are doing well. Better to have five to ten values that are remembered than fifteen that are forgotten.

Before you roll out a values set to the congregation, be sure you have lived with it long enough as leaders to know it communicates what you want. In my experience, it often takes three to six months of discussion, prayer, drafting, and redrafting before you say, "This is it."

MAKING VALUES MEANINGFUL

Many people are skeptical about identifying values because an organization's list of values often ends up in a file drawer, never again to see the light of day. Unfortunately, the habit of identifying and then filing values has bred cynicism as to their real worth. Intentional leaders take values seriously, recognizing that they keep ministry on course and out of weeds and shoals.

When values are inculcated at every level of ministry, they help bring common understanding to everyone in the congregation. This presupposes that leaders are personally committed to the values and are intentional about communicating them. The following points will help make your values meaningful—and keep them out of your filing cabinet.

Know your values. Here is a reason to keep the number of values to a minimum: Every leader, staff member, and volunteer needs to fully grasp them. Park your values in the constitution and bylaws, and they will be meaningless. Impress them on the minds of your key people, and they start to be lived out in ministry. Memorize them! The very fact that leaders and staff hold one another accountable for knowing the values makes a statement about the importance you attach to them.

Live your values. There is a great deal of cynicism about nonnegotiables today because too many people espouse one thing and live another—both in the Christian community and the marketplace. People watch leaders particularly, to see whether they take organizational values seriously.

As I mentioned, our workplace values teamwork, which means we will coordinate our efforts with others rather than allow silos and islands that do not cooperate. My staff team takes its cues from me on this. As I demonstrate teamwork and team attitudes with other leaders and departments, they do the same—even though this is not the natural tendency of departments.

Our management team has a policy that we will call one another on any violation of our values or mission. Values lived out by leaders will be the most powerful training tool for those we lead.

Communicate your values — constantly. Leaders underestimate the power of continually communicating values and overestimate how often they do it. One of a leader's primary jobs is creating the culture and ethos within which an organization is going to operate.

Senior pastors are the key (but not only) communicator. Some suggestions are to regularly weave the values into pulpit communication, tell stories of people who are living the values, explain how key decisions are made with values in mind, tie values into the scriptural text wherever possible (all congregational values should be linked to Scripture).

Many people will yawn when the senior pastor talks values. Here is the reason to persevere: Good values will help your church go where it needs to go. As you will see in chapter 14, most people are change-averse. Yet, leading often requires introducing change for the sake of missional fulfillment. If a congregation embraces the values, the senior pastor will be able to help them walk through change when necessary, because their commitment to shared values will be higher than their resistance to change.

All staff members ought to communicate values in their areas of leadership as well, tying their ministries to the values in a demonstrable way. Staff performance reviews and feedback for volunteers should include input on how well they are living out the values.

Values are also an important teaching tool for new attendees. They need to know the channel markers and ethos of your congregation.

Celebrate people and ministries that live out the values. People pay attention to what gets measured. Frequently highlighting examples of those who are living out the values will spur others to live them as well.

One of our organization's values is *Leadership: We take responsibility.* Not long ago, an administrative assistant took a call from a church and, during the conversation, discovered that its leaders were coming into town on a missions trip the same weekend as the NBA Final Four was there. There were no hotel rooms anywhere. Yet over the course of the day, she found the six hotel rooms needed. Beyond the call of duty? Actually, not. She was living out our values in a fabulous way. Needless to say, the rest of the staff heard the story, and she was a hero.

We constantly look for "God sightings"—times when God shows up because someone is living the mission. We celebrate those God sightings and encourage everyone to be on the lookout for ways they can live our mission and values.

Use values when hiring staff and selected leaders. Bill Hybels often talks of the "Three Cs" of team selection: character, competence, and chemistry.[4] A major part of chemistry is strong agreement with, and commitment to, your values.

Too often, in our desire to hire a staff member, we allow competence to trump either character or chemistry; the pain of that decision can be gut wrenching. Lack of values alignment will bring schism and conflict to your staff team that will eventually spread to the rest of the congregation. When hiring, I have begun a system of multiple interviews across my department, and often other departments, to ensure we are getting someone in alignment with our values and mission. If you have any question regarding buy-in of your values and culture, *don't hire*, no matter how qualified the applicant. Value alignment always trumps competence.

We should be equally concerned that board members are in alignment with our values. Many congregations don't even think to ask; later, they find themselves doing battle on the leadership level with someone who does not agree with the fundamental philosophy of the church.

DON'T NEGLECT YOUR CHANNEL MARKERS

The marinas along the Gulf of Florida and Alabama are full of boats that, through carelessness or accident, left the channel and lost their bottoms. Repairs are costly and expensive.

Intentional leaders carefully determine the channel markers that will guide their congregations. They vigilantly keep the ministry inside those markers and resist those who want to take the ministry into dangerous waters. Through their own example and clear communication, they ensure that everyone on the boat knows where those markers are and how to read them (it's a bad thing to get green and red markers mixed up!). Intentional leaders don't neglect their channel markers. They live by high-impact values.

H. I. MOMENT

What are our congregation's spoken and unspoken values? Which are healthy, and which are unhealthy?

Do we have written values, and are these values widely known, accepted, and lived out within the leadership, the staff team, and the wider congregation?

What can we do to ensure our values become widely held channel markers for all facets of our ministry?

H. I. WRAP-UP: THE VALUE OF VALUES

- Values are organizing principles for our ministries.
- Values bring alignment.
- Values rule out certain options.
- Values should be unique to your congregation.
- Values become intentional commitments by which congregations live.
- Your church culture is molded by your values.
- Values can be healthy or unhealthy.
- Values must be made meaningful through leaders, board, and staff communicating them and living them out.

Chapter Eight

MISSION: ESTABLISHING YOUR TRUE NORTH

If a congregation is to reach its God-given potential, leaders must have absolute mission clarity and an unwavering commitment to that mission. Mission clarity allows leaders to move a congregation in a specific direction that fulfills God's mandate for His church.

In the previous chapter, we saw that values establish the channel markers for our ministries. *Mission* answers the question, "Why do we exist?" and establishes specific direction. The ability to answer this question and help the entire congregation understand the answer is key to high-impact leadership and effective, healthy congregations.

Vagueness on mission leads to a diffusion of ministry effectiveness and competing, sometimes contradictory, directional pulls. The greater clarity we have for *why* we exist, the more focused our ministry energies can be. Mission does not answer questions of strategies a church will pursue. Rather, it answers an important directional question.

It is heartening to see the numbers of congregations—large and small, rural and urban—that are adopting mission statements that are clear and easy to understand and communicate. Through their mission statements, these congregations articulate the "main thing" for their churches.

THE MAIN THING

It's easy to forget the main thing because so many needs compete for our focus. Think of the issues faced on a regular basis in the typical congregation:

- A grieving family requires care after the loss of a loved one.
- The congregation is growing, and it looks inevitable that the church will have to expand, relocate, or rethink programming.
- Along with the expansion, the children's programs desperately need additional volunteers.
- A marriage is in trouble and requires extensive counseling.
- A conflict between members of the congregation is eating up the energies of the leadership board.
- The church is in a search process for a new staff member. In the meantime, they are short-staffed, requiring others to pick up the slack.
- A group in the church has "issues with the pastor's preaching" and wants to meet with the board.
- Income is not meeting budget, so leaders must decide where to cut.
- A great ministry opportunity to those recovering from divorce has opened up, and it will absorb the energies of several key leaders.

These are all important. Someone must deal with all of these. But is it possible that in addressing the many important things, we ignore the main thing—and miss the purpose for the church's existence? Having pastored and served in key leadership roles from a lay position, I have great sympathy for the nearly impossible demands placed on staff members and church leaders. I also know that unless we are able to keep the mission of the church in clear view, it is likely to be lost to the crisis of the moment.

JESUS DEFINED THE MAIN THING

Unlike other organizations, the main thing has already been defined for the local church. Jesus spelled it out in the Gospels, and the book of Acts reinforces it. The main thing is an extension of Jesus' own ministry, now to be carried out with the power of the Holy Spirit:

All authority in heaven and on earth has been given to me. Therefore go and make disciples of all nations, baptizing them in the name of the Father and of the Son and of the Holy Spirit, and teaching them to obey everything I have commanded you. And surely I am with you always, to the very end of the age. (Matthew 28:18-20)

The main thing here for the church is making disciples. The church's call, therefore, is to help people (wherever they are in their spiritual pilgrimage) understand the grace of Jesus, invite them to make Jesus their Lord and Savior, and help them grow into spiritual maturity until they are fully devoted followers of Jesus. At its most basic, the mission of the church is "more believers and better believers." It is being intentional in helping people who don't know Jesus to find a personal relationship with Him and then grow as a disciple.

HOW IS THE CHURCH DOING?

Some congregations are doing very well at keeping the main thing the main thing. But in general, the American church is not. Remember our earlier statistic: It takes one year and the efforts of eighty-five believers to bring just one person to Christ in the United States today.[1] At that rate, the U.S. church is growing more slowly than the general population. When it comes to developing fully devoted followers, studies show there is little difference in the lifestyles of believers versus the population as a whole. Fortunately, many congregations are seeing significant numbers of people come to Christ and are deeply intentional in their disciple-making process. These congregations, however, are a minority.

Why is the evangelical church not doing better at pursuing the main thing? I don't believe it is due to lack of concern or desire. In working with many leadership boards, I find that day-to-day demands distract us; the *important* keeps us from the *essential*. Mission drift takes place, and over time we forget why we exist. Eventually we are doing many good things, and it may even appear that we are doing well at the main thing. Yet it is easy to be fooled that we are operating by Christ's true north when we are not. For instance, it is possible for a congregation to grow rapidly due to its programming but have few conversions. If we are measuring by the Great Commission, the real measure is not congregational growth but conversion growth.

It is just as easy to be fooled in the arena of spiritual growth. If we measure success by programs or participation in programs, we may believe we are doing well. However, the measurement of spiritual growth is life change. Unless we can quantify major life change as members become more like Jesus, we may not be nearly as successful as we assume we are.

We have just lived through several decades in the United States where the emphasis among many church leaders was church growth or church size with *no real correlation* to either conversion growth or life change. Many pastors and lay leaders define success by the size, facility, and programming of their church. While this may be *one* definition of success, it has nothing to do with *Christ's* definition.

With eternal realities at stake, church leaders need to ask themselves:

- Is our church clear on its mission, and does our mission agree with the mission Jesus left the church in the Great Commission?
- Do all of our leaders and staff members agree our mission is the main thing, and are we all passionate about accomplishing that mission?
- Can we all clearly articulate our mission? How many in our congregation can articulate it?
- Can we measure with clarity, on an annual basis, how well we are doing in accomplishing the mission? Do we measure results honestly or simply assume we are doing well?
- Does our mission guide all the major initiatives and ministries of our church?
- What grade would we give our congregation on mission clarity and mission accomplishment?

Jesus gave us our true north in the Great Commission. By defining our mission in light of the one He left us, we have a guidance system that can keep us aligned with His calling.

DEVELOPING AND EVALUATING A MISSION STATEMENT

Whether you are developing a new mission statement or evaluating a current one, the following principles will be helpful in your process.

Craft it in alignment with the Great Commission. The mission statement should reflect the Great Commission priority of more believers and better believers, in language that is culturally relevant and easily understood.

Make it simple and clear. Here's the rule: If it can't be put on the back of a T-shirt, it's too long. If it requires a paragraph of explanation, it's too complex. If a whole congregation cannot memorize it easily, it needs work. If leaders don't know it, it's useless. As you develop your mission statement, give it sufficient time to percolate among leaders so you can refine, simplify, and clarify. It's amazing how a bit of time, discussion, prayer, and thought can edit a complex statement into a simple one.

Be specific. The more general your statement, the less helpful it will be as a compass. For instance, "The mission of Christ Church is to bring glory to God" is theologically correct but so nonspecific that it is of little use as a directional tool. On the other hand, "The mission of Christ Church is to bring God glory by lovingly introducing people to Jesus and helping them grow in Him" is far more focused. It includes evangelism, spiritual growth, and a climate of love. These can each be measured.

Be sure it's yours. Be wary of taking someone else's mission statement and adopting it for your congregation. Most likely the statement will reflect another church's situation. Allow God to be creative through *your* leadership to develop a statement that is true to your context and in alignment with His Great Commission.

Ask, "Can I get excited about the mission?" Leaders should take seriously the true-north nature of their mission. They need to embrace the mission with passion and rigorously resolve to keep the church on course. Passion comes from believing this is the mission for *your* church, something you as a leader are willing to follow long term. If you as a leader can't get excited about your mission, others won't either. If you are passionate about it, others will be too.

The problem with mission statements is not usually with the mission itself but the commitment of leaders to embrace it, live it, and evaluate adherence to it. When prayerfully and carefully developed, passionately embraced, and intentionally lived out, your mission becomes the directional compass for your ministry.

LIVING THE MISSION

Mission becomes meaningful to the extent that people understand it, believe it, and begin to live it. Everyone should be invited to live the mission, but all staff members, leaders, and volunteers must be *committed* to doing so.

How does a well-defined mission affect the decision-making of church leaders, staff members, and volunteers? Let's go back to that of Christ Church: "The mission of Christ Church is to bring God glory by lovingly introducing people to Jesus and helping them grow in Him."

Christ Church is committed to three things regardless of the many other good things it may do: evangelism, intentional spiritual maturity, and a climate of love. As Christ Church's leaders evaluate ministries in light of this commitment, these are the kinds of questions they would ask:

- Are we seeing evidence of people coming to Christ, or is our growth simply transfer growth?
- What pieces of our ministry contribute directly to evangelism? Should additional resources, people, or budgets be directed toward our evangelism efforts?
- How well have we defined what spiritual maturity looks like so we know our target? (See chapter 3.)
- How are we doing, as we measure spiritual growth? What weak spots do we need to concentrate on? Are we pleased with our intentionality in this part of our ministry?
- What are the evidences that the congregation is displaying God's love to one another and to outsiders in a healthy way? How can we apply this part of our mission to the inner city that's only five blocks from our campus?
- Could we help our people resolve differences in a more biblical fashion so that God's love is not spoiled by unresolved issues?
- Does this new program being proposed, or this staff restructuring, help or detract from our main mission?

My assumption is that Christ Church has a variety of good ministries consistent with its DNA. By paying close attention to the mission, its leaders are able to keep the congregation pointed toward true north. Whatever Christ Church undertakes, the church stays on target by being clear on its mission and paying diligent attention to it.

One essential step involves requiring all ministries of the church to integrate the mission in tangible ways. Consider the children's ministry of our fictional Christ Church. Because the church's mission is about evangelism, spiritual growth, and loving relationships, the children's ministry would be asked to integrate these three elements. Staff members would therefore emphasize evangelism opportunities, intentional spiritual growth for children, and fostering loving relationships as they train volunteers and plan programs.

Multiply this strategy to youth, music, senior ministries, caring, and every other ministry, and soon you have a whole church playing in the same symphony—each with different instruments, but all tuned to the same key.

Mission alignment must be a nonnegotiable for every staff member and volunteer leader. No matter how strong people's giftedness, they should not be a player in your symphony if they are not aligned with your mission. Multiple missions mean multiple agendas, so be lovingly clear to all leaders that mission alignment is a requirement.

A simple way to ensure this alignment is to ask all ministry leaders to fill out an annual ministry plan that includes how they will integrate the mission into their ministries. If your congregation has a small-group ministry, consider challenging every small group to think of concrete ways of contributing to the mission of the church.

As the staff and leaders begin to align with and live out the mission, it must also be communicated to the congregation.

COMMUNICATING THE MISSION

Several years ago I saw a commercial showing a bunch of tough-looking cowboys riding the plains, lariats whipping. You could just picture the herd of cattle charging in front of them. Then the camera turned to the herd, and I saw thousands of cats running in every different direction, with the Marlboro men in hot pursuit. I immediately thought, *That's a picture of the church.* It perfectly captured the reality of a bunch of independent folks from every conceivable background come to church, and as God's cowboys, we try to convince them they ought to be running in the same direction without clawing at one another or biting us. (Okay, so I'm a bit pragmatic about church leadership!)

Now, neither people nor cats are going to go in the same direction in an *orderly* fashion, but we've done a lot if we can at least get them heading in the same *general* direction. This is where mission—when constantly and clearly communicated in a variety of ministry settings—becomes a powerful directional tool.

As you regularly communicate your church's truth north, people start to assimilate it into their thinking. Willow Creek Community

Church has a well-known mission statement: "To turn irreligious people into fully devoted followers of Jesus Christ." You cannot be around the church for very long without knowing it. As a result, the church has had tremendous impact on many lives. Willow Creek has defined its mission, is passionate about its mission, lives its mission, and actively communicates its mission.

When a church does that, it calls its people beyond ordinary living to their unique place in God's compelling mission.

CELEBRATING AN EXCITING MISSION

People ask, "Is there more to life than my job, my paycheck, my four-by-four, my golf game?" The answer is a huge divine *yes*. The best part of waking up is not Folgers in my cup; it's the Holy Spirit in my heart and another divine call to represent Jesus to an empty and dying world.

Our people need to understand they are the ultimate players in God's divine drama. God has commissioned us to be His representatives to a hurting world, thrown in His divine gifts so we can do it well, and invested us with His own Spirit in us so we have His supernatural power as we carry out His work. Then He said, "I'll be with you every step of the way." There is no higher call than to be engaged in God's kingdom work. When we help people understand they can give up their petty dreams for God-sized dreams, we capture their hearts with the call of Jesus to join Him in changing the world. This is why communicating a compelling mission is so important.

Let's be frank for a moment. Too many churches exist with small and mundane ministry dreams that don't excite anyone—leaders or congregation. If we cannot give our people a biblically grounded, exhilarating reason to become engaged with God, then we have failed as leaders and we have failed God and our people.

Boring dreams elicit boredom and nonengagement. Yet the Gospels tell us that every time someone on earth trusts in Christ, heaven throws a party. We need to be throwing more parties, celebrating the mission God has given us and the victories along the way. Have you ever noticed the number of times the apostle Paul broke into a spontaneous doxology of thanks to God in his epistles? Or how grateful he was to be part of God's divine drama of salvation? We must think deeply, as Paul did, about the call upon our lives and the ministry Christ has graciously given to us, and then call our people to accept Christ's invitation.

I remember the day the White House called my brother to ask for his help in the president's faith-based initiative. Actually, his business partner took the call and didn't believe it was the White House calling, so he told them to call back on his cell phone. They did — to his surprise (and perhaps embarrassment). Two days later they were in a meeting with the president.

Heady stuff.

Guess what? God has called. Did we hear it? Are we communicating that call with more enthusiasm and passion than we would if the White House had called?

Great church leaders have heard God's call, have defined their mission, and are constantly challenging their people to answer the call. They are helping their people dream God-sized dreams for their congregation and sign on for life-changing work. They are helping their people celebrate the astonishing invitation to join Him in His work. They are excited, and they excite their people.

TELL STORIES

Mission comes alive when people can see it in action rather than view it as words on paper. A celebration/baptism service with stories about how people found Christ is far more powerful than simple exhortations to share the good news. Consider these stories:

- One congregation prayed for five hundred people to come to Christ through its direct ministry in one year. It happened — and they were a congregation of fewer than five hundred people.
- At another church, someone stood and told the congregation about having been deeply involved in pornography before

finding freedom. This account of spiritual growth was more powerful than any sermon a pastor could have given on the subject.

- A businesswoman gathered a group of executives in her industry to pray for ways to reach their colleagues. Her story motivated other professionals to think of ways they could influence their peers.
- Young people "lived the mission" by giving two weeks of their summer to inner-city ministry and developing a heart for others.
- A high school student established a weekly small group for his non-Christian friends. They talked, studied Scripture, and played paintball together.

Great leaders constantly tell stories such as these to illustrate their mission. And they ask those whose lives have been touched to tell their stories. Through regular storytelling, leaders unpack the implications of their mission, helping people contextualize and apply that mission to their situations. Most opportunities to fulfill the mission will be found where we spend most of our week—at school, at work, in our neighborhoods, through Little League, and at barbecues with our friends.

Stories and examples spur people on. Help people dream dreams about how they can live the mission in their spheres of influence. Let them know that they—not the pastoral staff—are the key to the mission's fulfillment. The church comes together once (or twice) a week to be equipped, motivated, and encouraged so they can do the church's work as God's ambassadors the other six days.

TRUE NORTH MATTERS

Mission is about understanding the true north for your congregation and helping your people live that mission. Without a true north, many directions become possible, diffusing effectiveness, energy, and focus. A carefully crafted and lived mission is the most powerful tool any organization can use to bring alignment to a large number of people and help them move in the same general direction.

A biblically consistent mission also brings people into alignment with God's mission for the church. If the church is going to influence its community, large numbers of people need to live out the Great Commission.

Congregations that are doing well have a simple, well-defined mission statement that serves as the compass to keep them on true north. By constantly referring to the reason for their existence, they allow their mission to keep them moving in the right direction, and they correct "mission drift" when it occurs. All ministries of the church can be evaluated against true north; all staff members can be held account-able for their contribution to true north; all volunteers can be brought into alignment with the mission.

Once you have determined your general direction, you are ready to consider vision, or your preferred future.

H. I. MOMENT

Are we satisfied with our church's current mission statement? Does it meet the criteria for a good mission statement?

Am I personally motivated and excited about it? If so, why? If not, why not?

How many who attend our church could tell us the mission of the church? Are they passionate about the mission?

Do all leaders, staff members, and key volunteers buy into and live consistent with the mission? If not, what do we need to do to bring alignment?

What could we be doing better to ensure that the mission is known, understood, and passionately pursued by our congregation?

H. I. WRAP-UP: MISSION

- Mission clarifies to your congregation why you exist; it answers the question, "What is our main thing?"
- Your mission is a teaching tool with your congregation as to the purpose of the church.
- Your mission should help your congregation stay in alignment with the Great Commission that Christ left the church.
- Clarity on mission allows leaders to evaluate whether your congregation is aligned with your true north on a regular basis.

Chapter Nine

VISION: BREAKING INTO THE FUTURE

A great deal of confusion surrounds the word *vision*. For many, it conjures up ephemeral ideas that are hard to pin down and even harder to define. This is especially true if you are not one of those natural-born leaders who seems able to articulate vision at the drop of a hat. The common question is, "How do you define vision?"

In this chapter, I want to demythologize vision and provide some simple ways your congregation can clarify where it wants to go in the future.

YOUR PREFERRED FUTURE

Vision answers the question, "Where are we going as a congregation?" It defines your preferred future for your ministry over the next three to five years. To go back to the analogy of the two houses, your vision or preferred future is analogous to the blueprint Grant and Carol drew up for their home. Unless you are Sarah Winchester, you do not build a home without a plan. Yet many ministries exist for decades without a clear directional plan.

Scripture gives us many examples of the power of vision. In the Old Testament, Ezra led a remnant of the Israelites out of exile in Persia and back to Jerusalem. But once they got there, he didn't know what to do next. He had no clear direction. As a result, the people existed for many years in less-than-favorable conditions, unable to rebuild the city or even protect their crops. Church-health statistics indicate many congregations today also cannot answer the question, "What next?" The result is that, as in Ezra's time, ministry languishes in a holding pattern.

Contrast the condition under Ezra with that under Nehemiah. Nehemiah was deeply troubled when he heard of the state of his people, and after spending considerable time in prayer, he decided to act. Nehemiah's vision included the physical rebuilding of the city wall and the spiritual renewal of a disheartened people. Unlike Ezra, Nehemiah had a blueprint for rebuilding the literal and spiritual walls, and he systematically set about carrying out that plan.

Healthy and vital ministries know where they are going. They have worked to clarify their preferred future and are systematically moving the congregation *into* that future (we'll talk about that in the next chapter). They are building ministry according to a blueprint rather than without. Clarity about where a ministry is going makes a clear difference between healthy, vital, and growing ministries and those that are not.

TRUTHS ABOUT VISION

As we begin to talk about developing a vision for our preferred future, there are several principles we need to keep in mind.

Planning is compatible with letting God lead. For some, particularly those who lean toward the spiritualist end of the spectrum, talking about planning for the future of ministry is antithetical to allowing God to lead and seeing where He takes us. Yet all of us live with a vision of our preferred *personal* future. We save for homes we want to purchase; we plan for retirement; we think of ways to build into our marriages and children. I am continually trying to help my two sons think through their plans for the future, knowing that wise choices now will dramatically influence their options later. None of this planning precludes God's direction along the way, but it certainly allows for a wiser, more orderly life with greater opportunities.

Each church has a unique genetic code and a unique vision. As we explored in chapter 5, every congregation has a unique DNA. Thus, it is a mistake to assume that you can import the vision of another church. Your preferred future will be a composite of factors unique to you:

- The community in which you reside
- The gifts within your congregation
- The gifts of your staff members and senior pastor
- The resources available to you
- Ministry opportunities God has provided and where you have had success
- Your church's cultural and ethnic makeup
- The generational groups within your congregation
- The size of your congregation
- The ministry philosophy you embrace
- Your areas of strength
- How God is leading your congregation

What *is* the same for all congregations is the mission spelled out in the Great Commission. How each congregation works out the Great Commission will be different. This is why we cannot replicate the methodology or vision of other churches we admire (often high-profile congregations). We can learn from them, but we are not them. Often, the single most important thing successful ministries can teach us is the importance of vision, direction, and intentionality—because they specialize in it!

It is as we discover how God has made *us*—and then explore the opportunities we have—that we will flourish and grow.

Vision is not about size and numbers. The preferred future for your congregation is about reaching the maximum potential God has for the next phase of your ministry. That may include size and numbers because deciding to focus on the spiritual health of your congregation will generally bring both spiritual and numerical growth. But size and numbers aren't the purpose. Vision is about maximizing your opportunities, the spiritual growth and health of your congregation, the ministry impact of your church, and other factors you believe are important.

A vision provides a working document, not an inflexible rule. It is rare that no changes are made to a building's blueprints after they are completed. As Grant and Carol were building their home, each Monday morning there was a site meeting among them, the builder, and the architect. The group dealt with issues as they surfaced and made modifications along the way. The house's basic structure remained the same, but details changed.

The same is true for your church. Vision or preferred future gives you a good framework. But it is a working plan, allowing for flexibility when necessary and for God's Spirit to break in with new insights. Your preferred future is a working document on the direction you want to chart, not an expertly crafted constitution or bylaw-like document. It can be changed; it can be modified; and it will be.

GETTING TO YOUR PREFERRED FUTURE

If you have never done this before, I encourage you to keep the process of creating a vision simple and uncomplicated. Before you start, ask yourself who needs to be in the discussion. I would certainly include your staff members, key leadership, and other ministry influencers in the church. The more people you involve on the front end, the more buy-in you will have on the back end.

Remind those involved that the discussion is not about how you have done things in the past. It is about clarifying where the ministry will go in the next phase. In three to five years, you will need to repeat this exercise because your ministry and your community will both have changed. We honor the past and periodically reenvision the future. This will help those who have ownership in past ministries feel better about envisioning the future.

Because you are looking at a three- to five-year time frame here, you want a balance between faith and reality in your discussions. Just as you would not ask an architect to design a million-dollar home for a $200,000 budget, you do not want to craft unrealistic dreams for your ministry. At the same time, you are envisioning the future based on God's blessing, so—within reason—you don't want money to be a limiting factor. Make plans consistent with who you are and the resources you have—but stretch yourself a bit too, as Nehemiah did.

I recommend you first talk through some of the factors that form your ministry's unique composite (see the bulleted list above). Start by thinking about how God has formed and gifted your congregation and the opportunities you already see for ministry. Answer the question, "Who are we today, and what opportunities are available to maximize our spiritual influence over the next three to five years?" Have someone document your discussions for future reference.

Second, review your mission and values to make sure these important principles inform your discussion. Anything you decide about your preferred future must be consistent with your mission and values—although this discussion may well prompt you to revisit both.

Third—and here is the heart of your work—take a few hours or a few meetings with a whiteboard to answer this question: "Given what we know about ourselves, our opportunities, our community, and our genetic code, what do we believe God would be pleased for our congregation to look like in three to five years if He blesses and if money is not an issue?"

In answering this question, consider these categories (and add others you believe are important):

- Spiritual climate of the church
- Relationships in the church
- Staffing for ministry
- Outreach opportunities
- Missions ministries
- Ministries to the poor and disadvantaged
- Facilities for ministry
- Community impact
- Leadership development
- Deployment of people in ministry
- Financial stewardship
- Youth, children's, and specialized ministries

As you brainstorm, you'll realize that your leaders may have ministry dreams in their hearts that they have never put into words. You will also see that there are many common dreams!

Having done this, assign your best writer to do an initial draft that summarizes your preferred future under common themes. This should not be more than a two-page document. Circulate the document among the participants and ask them if it generally expresses the direction they envision. After feedback, do a second and third draft as needed.

Within three to six months, you should be able to reach a consensus on a preferred-future document. (The larger the church, the more time this takes because of the number of leaders and staff members involved.) Again, because this is a working document, you don't need perfection. You do need clarity. Wherever possible, include measurable statements rather than general statements so that leadership can determine progress each year.

Before you finish, use a meeting or series of meetings to explain the process and goal to your congregation and allow them to dream with you. One church invited people to gather at tables of ten to twelve people to dream together about the future and then posted the results around the auditorium for everyone to read over a period of weeks.

As you are able, incorporate the congregation's feedback into your final working document. You will discover that many in your congregation have great vision and are longing for your church to be more intentional in its ministry direction. Dreams engender vision; vision creates excitement; and excitement and vision translate into ministry energy! In this way, your preferred future becomes a powerful ministry tool.

VISION BRINGS DIRECTION AND FOCUS

Not only does this tool capture energy, it answers the question of direction. A vision gives you a working framework by which to make decisions. It allows you to focus on what you believe is important and to say no to ministry options that are not consistent with who you are and where you want to go. Consider the following examples of churches whose vision documents gave them direction for their plans.

I recently met with two leaders of a small church in Hong Kong that has a vision for reaching the rest of Asia with the gospel. With fewer than one hundred members, this church is investing large sums of money and energy in countries closed to traditional missions and is helping train hundreds of church planters through highly leveraged and strategic means. Because Asian outreach is central to their preferred future, they have captured the imagination of their small congregation and created tremendous excitement for what God is doing in the countries around them, and they are challenging individuals to give in a sacrificial way. While this is not their only priority as a church, it is a major directional decision. Their focus results in channeling creative energy for the Great Commission.

Another dynamic and rapidly growing ministry in Madison, Wisconsin, has a huge outreach to students at the University of Wisconsin. Because God has opened up this significant ministry door, ministering to students has become a major part of their vision. A few years ago, when faced with space issues, they had to decide whether to build on their current property, relocate, or develop a second campus. Their preferred future of ministering to university students drove their decision not to abandon their geographical area—even though space there is hard to find. Everyone at this church knows ministry to university students is a significant part of their vision, so their preferred future drives key decisions.

In Knoxville, Tennessee, Two Rivers Church has committed to helping the poor in its community as a key part of its preferred future. Two Rivers is the church we mentioned earlier that, when it raised money for its first permanent facility, tithed a portion of everything raised to local ministries that ministered among the disadvantaged.

In each of these cases, the preferred future of the congregation played a key role in decisions and congregational focus. If the churches hadn't had clarity of vision, they might have made vastly different decisions.

The flip side of the coin is that clarity of direction rules out certain options as well. For leaders, decision-making is vastly easier when they know where they want to go—and where they do not want to go.

AN EXAMPLE OF ONE CONGREGATION'S PREFERRED FUTURE

The following is a preferred-future or vision document from a church of about three hundred. The multigenerational, blue- and white-collar congregation meets in a less-than-ideal facility in a suburban area. It has significant leadership and financial resources for a church its size.

The document answers the question, "What do we want to look like in ten years if God blesses and if money is not an issue?" The congregation's leadership is committed to move systematically toward this preferred future over the next decade. As you read this church's vision document, try to envision the kind of culture and ministry priorities the leaders might desire to build during the next phase of the church's existence.

OUR VISION

Believing that God would have us be intentional in our ministry and maximize our potential as a church in line with the gifts and opportunities He has given us, the following represents what we believe God would be pleased for our church to look like in ten years if He blesses and provides financially.

It is our dream to be a congregation filled with grace and love, a place of safety and acceptance for visitors and members alike, where the love of Jesus is so compelling that it draws seekers into a life-changing fellowship of believers. Because love for one another and for those who don't yet know Christ is the key quality of believers, we will do all we can to encourage relational health and unity — with an emphasis on the twin concepts of grace and truth.

It is our dream to be a church known in its community for its good deeds and care for the people around us. So we will intentionally focus much of our energy on meeting needs of those around us as well as those in our greater geographic area. We will focus particularly on the poor, the needy, the forgotten, and the hurting — meeting real needs and thereby demonstrating in tangible ways the love and care of Jesus Christ.

It is our dream to be intentionally involved in sharing the good news of Jesus in our local community, our region, our nation, and our world. We will therefore allocate our financial, staff, and volunteer resources in a way that targets these three geographic areas for missions, compassion projects, and on-site ministry teams. It is our goal to see at least 10 percent of our congregation involved in hands-on short-term missions projects annually and every small group involved in a community project annually. We will pay special attention to ministry to the needy, disenfranchised, and hurting as we pursue a missions strategy.

It is our dream to multiply the influence of God in surrounding communities by intentionally planting daughter congregations throughout the northwest metro area where we are situated. We will be generous in providing resources and people to plant these congregations, believing that God blesses those who share His values.

It is our dream to be a church where people are connected with others in authentic community for growth, care, and fellowship. We will focus on developing small groups where transparency, truth, love, and care are present and where all adults who call our church their home can grow in their spiritual lives. We want to be a church *of* small groups, not a church *with* small groups.

It is our dream to become a large regional church having an impact on the whole northwest quadrant of our metro area. We intend to relocate to property we already own on a major freeway and build a facility that will preserve our ministry options long into the future. We desire this facility to be inviting to the unchurched, to be accessible to all social groups, to be user-friendly, and to be a place where ministries to all ages (and especially to families) can take place.

It is our dream to minister in a multigenerational context. We intend to provide worship options that will meet the various needs of people within our church and community. This will mean different worship styles and a flexible strategy that can minister to a variety of generations and preferences. Because of our commitment to ministering to families, we will pay special attention to the quality of our children's and youth ministries. Our goal is to develop a great full-time staff team that will, in turn, develop, empower, and release others in meaningful, multigenerational ministry.

It is our dream to be a congregation of people who use their God-given gifts in service both inside and outside the church. We will help all individuals within our congregation identify their God-given gifts and help them find ways to use these gifts for the advancement of the kingdom. We believe that it is only as all members are "in the game" and involved in ministry that the body will be everything God has called us to be.

It is our dream that the end result of our ministry together is that all of us become fully devoted followers of Jesus Christ. Thus we will be intentional in helping all individuals who call this their church home to be people who understand and live in the grace of Christ, who are regularly growing in their followership of Jesus Christ, who are involved in the fellowship of a small group, who are using their God-given gifts and abilities for the growth of His kingdom, and who are honoring God with their resources.

It is our dream to maximize the health and ministry impact of our congregation by empowering godly leaders to lead well. We will always ensure that our church structures are leadership-friendly and reflect the size of the congregation and the leadership needs. We intend to be mission-driven in our leadership and will change our systems as needed to ensure that we have an empowered church for our board, our staff members, and our volunteers.

VISION AS A BLUEPRINT

Before Grant and Carol could start building their home on the river bluff in Wisconsin, they needed to translate their values and mission for that home into a blueprint. That is what your picture of the preferred future is: a blueprint for the future of your ministry. Your vision statement is literally a word picture of where you believe God desires your church to go in the next three to five years. Once you have a blueprint, you can then move to the next step: intentionally building toward that future via ministry initiatives that can turn your dreams into reality. But don't start building without your blueprint.

H. I. MOMENT

What are the commitments of the church leaders who crafted the sample "Our Vision" document above?

Do we have a good picture of where we believe our church should be going in the next three to five years?

Does our congregation know where we are headed?

What work do we need to do as leaders to help clarify our church's preferred future? When will we schedule time as a leadership community to do this?

H. I. WRAP-UP: VISION

- Vision answers the question, "Where are we going as a congregation?"
- Vision is your preferred future.
- Your preferred future is influenced by your congregation's unique genetic code.
- Your preferred future becomes a working document, like a set of architectural blueprints, for where you desire to see the congregation go.
- Your vision is based on what you believe God would be pleased to see your congregation accomplish in the next three to five years.
- Vision brings direction and focus to future planning.

Chapter Ten

INITIATIVES: TRANSLATING DREAMS INTO REALITY

Determining our preferred future is critical, but it makes little difference unless we can translate our dreams into action. If the construction company Grant and Carol hired could not turn blueprints into a beautiful and functional home, Prairie Ledge would have remained a dream, an unfulfilled plan.

It is precisely at this point of translation into action that many leadership boards stall out. They have dreams, but they are frustrated by their inability to bring those dreams to fruition. A crucial difference between vibrant, healthy, growing churches and those that have not fulfilled their God-given potential is the discipline of systematically getting the right things to move them toward their preferred future.

I am frequently asked during consultations, "How *do* we actually get stuff done?" This chapter will explore a simple way you can move the ministry ball down the field on a consistent basis.

HOW DOES PROGRESS HAPPEN?

Forward movement toward a preferred future happens when leaders choose to tackle a few ministry initiatives on an annual basis. *A ministry initiative is an action step that will take significant time, money, energy, or congregational buy-in over a one- to three-year period, resulting in a major move toward a preferred future.* Examples of ministry initiatives include:

- Hiring key staff members
- Launching a building campaign or relocation effort
- Initiating a network of small groups throughout the congregation
- Changing the church governance system
- Founding a comprehensive care program
- Starting a new ministry or redesigning a current ministry
- Formulating a disciple-making plan to move people toward spiritual maturity
- Initiating significant community services

Let me offer a real-life example of a ministry initiative. We'll refer back to this example later as we consider helpful principles of choosing and implementing initiatives.

EXAMPLE OF A MINISTRY INITIATIVE

Initiative: To develop a comprehensive small-group structure for adults within our congregation. The structure will be designed to promote life change, relational connectedness, and care. Small-group involvement is to become one of five commitments we ask of all adult attendees because we believe it is critical to our members experiencing life change and relational wholeness. Our goal is to have 80-plus percent of our adults committed to a weekly small group.

Champion: Bill Williamson (staff)
Time frame: 24 months
Accountability: senior pastor

Plan Outline

September–December 2006. Recruit several key staff members and volunteers to work with Bill toward launching small groups in September 2007. Research the best models of small groups in other churches around the country to determine whether there are models we can emulate. Find out from leaders of model small-group ministries what worked for them, what didn't, and what they would have done differently.

January 12, 2007. Report findings to leadership board.

January–June 2007. In order to pave the way for this change in congregational life, senior pastor uses multiple opportunities from the pulpit and in writing to explain the benefits of the upcoming small groups and the goal of 80 percent involvement.

January–March 2007. Bill discusses research results with staff team and comes up with a proposed model for the church. Determine with staff members what modifications should be made to chosen model to best fit the needs and preferred future of the congregation.

April–June 2007. Bill recruits the fifteen small-group leaders who will be needed in September.

April 24, 2007. Board meeting with Bill, small-group committee, and staff team to discuss specifics of small-group proposal. Final decision to be made in May.

May 25, 2007. Board finalizes decision.

June–August 2007. Bill conducts several training sessions for small-group leaders. Information is passed out to all church members, sign-up tables are set up on Sundays, and leaders recruit people to their groups.

September 12, 2007. Church kickoff of small groups with a celebration and additional recruitment.

September 2007–May 2008. Bill and his team monitor quality of small groups, offer ongoing training, recruit additional leaders for September 2008, and communicate progress to church leaders. Move toward goal of folding all new church attendees into small groups and reaching 80 percent congregational involvement. Bill and senior pastor meet monthly to discuss any issues and review number of adults attending. Board receives monthly numbers and percentages of adults attending small groups.

May 2008. Debrief with board on start-up of small-group ministry. Evaluate current status and percentage-to-goal of those attending. Initiative is completed, but small-group ministry will continue under Bill's leadership with a monthly report to board and senior pastor of percentage of adults involved.

DEVELOPING A MINISTRY INITIATIVE

Keep this example of a ministry initiative in mind as you read the following principles. Together, they will help you choose wisely and execute your key initiatives well.

Consider your preferred future. Just as the blueprints for Prairie Ledge guided the construction company as it translated the dream into reality, so the vision or preferred future for your ministry becomes the basis for your initiatives.

Before Rick Warren planted Saddleback Church, he had an audacious vision (preferred future). Those familiar with his book *The Purpose-Driven Church* know Saddleback Church has substantially fulfilled this God-sized vision over two decades of ministry. While its methods were unique and creative (like those of most vibrant ministries), one of the main reasons for the church's success is that strategic decisions were always tied to where the church wanted to go, who it wanted to be, and the ministry impact it desired. Church leaders formed a clear purpose, and their ministry decisions were driven by that vision.

This is true of most healthy, vibrant, growing churches. While church leaders often look to these cutting-edge congregations for useful ministry methods, we forget the most important lesson they can teach us: They have a picture of where they want to go, and all major ministry decisions are made on the basis of that blueprint.

Remember: Less is more. In any given year, leaders must answer a key question: "What do we do next?" There is no shortage of things churches *could* do, nor is there any shortage of things people *think* they should do. Frequently, boards are frustrated and even paralyzed by the available options.

Churches that tackle too many issues at once will find they do not complete most of them adequately. The smaller a church, the more important it is to limit the number of ministry initiatives you tackle, so you can do them well. Choosing what to do next requires hard work, discipline, and God's wisdom. This is what leaders do.

The more specific question that leaders (both elected leaders and staff members) must answer is: "If we can only do three to five truly significant things this year, and at this time in our ministry, which ones will move us closer to our preferred future?" Framing the question this way forces leaders to prioritize their options based on their chosen future and the stage of ministry in which they find themselves.

In answering this question, leaders also need to consider whether they have the time, personnel, or resources to complete the initiatives successfully. If, for instance, a desired initiative requires significant staff leadership, but no staff member has the time or expertise to carry it out, the staffing issue must be solved before the initiative is launched. At times, you will conclude that it is better to wait on an initiative until you have the ability to execute it well.

Once an initiative has been decided on and there is agreement among leaders and staff members, everyone needs the discipline not to add additional key initiatives until the current ones have been completed. This is all about leading intentionally rather than haphazardly!

A few key initiatives, rightly chosen, will drive you further down the road than numerous small initiatives that merely tweak your ministry. Remember, your preferred future is a long-term blueprint for a ministry that will be built one key initiative at a time.

Choose a champion, a plan, and a timeline. Leaders are commonly frustrated by how often well-intentioned plans never come to reality or how they drag on without significant progress. Good intentions are not enough; results matter if we are to be all God wants us to be.

Achieving results starts with the clear designation of the person responsible for driving an initiative to completion. Murky accountability yields murky results. Further, initiatives do not succeed when they are driven by committee. The designated champion—whether a board member, staff member, or volunteer—needs to be clear on his or her responsibility and willing to ensure that the initiative is completed. Therefore, in choosing champions for initiatives, be sure they have proven ability as well as margin for availability.

Ask your champion to come up with a plan for accomplishing the initiative, including specific time parameters attached to key milestones (see the plan on pages 150–151 for an example). The plan may not include what the completed initiative will look like (you probably will not know this), but it must be specific enough to instill confidence that you can move from an ideal to a completed product over the next one to three years.

After church leaders have signed off on the plan and provided the necessary resources, they must add the new initiative to future agendas, creating added accountability for driving the initiative to completion.

Cultivate a culture of accountability. Church boards and staff teams are notorious for not holding individuals (including themselves) accountable for results or for not keeping agreed-on commitments. Our cultures of "nice" and "conflict avoidance" and "this is ministry" often get in the way of our desires for excellence and ministry results. As a result, accountability for results is not fostered; initiatives do not get completed; and ministry suffers.

Intentional ministry is only possible when leaders and staff members are committed to the discipline of getting things done with appropriate accountability. Keeping promises, meeting deadlines, executing with excellence, understanding priorities, and implementing plans are all part of a culture of accountability — crucial to the health and effectiveness of your ministry.

As you review the earlier example of a ministry initiative, note the built-in accountability. Even before the board signs off on this initiative, everyone knows the milestones for review and decision-making.

At the same time, Bill (who wrote the plan) has given himself adequate time to complete the steps he knows will be required for its successful completion. The senior pastor, as Bill's supervisor, will monitor Bill's progress through regular meetings. Then, an evaluation of the program is scheduled at the end of the two years, along with a review of the percentage of adults involved in small groups as compared to the goal. Finally, through the monthly reports to the staff team and the board, Bill has built-in incentive to ensure the involvement goal continues to be met.

Include measurable results. A factor in developing a culture of discipline and results is measuring your key indicators of success. All ministry initiatives need to be measured if they are going to be meaningful. What you measure is what people will pay attention to; what is not measured is usually not considered important. In our example, the measurement was the percentage of adults participating in small groups. The congregation, Bill, and the leadership board all understood what spelled success. If the initiative had not included measurements, there would have been no way to know if it had succeeded.

Be flexible when situations change. Builders follow blueprints carefully. But blueprints are subject to change when, in the process of building, flaws are discovered in the plan or what was planned is not going to work. While following the general blueprint, don't be shy about tweaking it as needed or as circumstances change.

Aim for closure and evaluation. Initiatives should have specific start and end dates. When an initiative has been successfully completed, celebrate the milestone together. Thank the champion and those involved in a tangible way. Don't move on without a celebration and a thank-you.

Closure also involves evaluation against the measurable parameters. Don't ignore missed goals. Where goals were not met, leadership needs to discuss why it happened and what the board, staff member, or champion could have done differently. If you set an unrealistic goal, acknowledge it. If the champion executed poorly, discuss it. If the congregation was not on the same page (or the leadership misread them), be honest about it. Takeaway lessons are only valid if you face them.

An evaluation should also be made of the formation and execution of the initiative itself. Questions such as "How could we have written the initiative better?" and "What did we learn in the process?" can inform future initiatives. Have your champion participate in these discussions so you capture his or her insights firsthand. Put these observations in writing so you don't forget lessons learned and ways you can better execute initiatives.

The more you do this, the more likely it is that you will continue to see initiatives successfully completed, because you are developing a culture of execution and accountability.

H. I. MOMENT

When a church culture lacks accountability and good execution, decisions often must be made again and again. How would you characterize your church culture toward concrete decision-making, carry-through, and accountability? Does this area require more discipline in your ministry?

H. I. BEST PRACTICE

Never neglect evaluating a ministry initiative. A healthy learning environment always considers what went right, what went wrong, what could have been done differently, and what lessons can be learned for the future. This is called "autopsy without blame." Learning organizations are not interested in blaming, but in growing.

DEVELOP AN ANNUAL RHYTHM FOR INITIATIVES

Accountability, execution, and prioritizing of next initiatives take place best on an annual rhythm. Because church years are normally centered on the school year, consider starting new initiatives in September and planning on a one- to three-year time frame. Some initiatives do not depend on the ministry year and can be initiated at any time.

Whatever your starting point, church leaders and senior staff need an annual touch point when they answer the question, "What initiatives have we completed this year, and what initiatives do we need next in order to move closer to our preferred future?"

I strongly recommend boards do this in an annual two- to three-day retreat held at the same time each year. While planning goes on throughout the year, this annual retreat is an opportunity for you as board members to:

- Evaluate core values of the church and discuss whether they are consistently lived out. If the values are not being lived out, what needs to be done to bring the congregation into alignment with the stated values?
- Discuss the mission of the church and whether the congregation

understands and is living the mission.

- Remind yourselves of the vision or preferred future, spending time on each section and asking, "Where have we made progress in the past year?" Without redoing the document (unless you need to reenvision it), ask, "Has God shown us anything in the past year that ought to be part of our preferred future?"
- Evaluate the progress of your current ministry initiatives. Celebrate and keep a running record of completed initiatives. Thank God for progress made and milestones passed in the previous year.
- Identify the next initiatives needed to drive your ministry closer to the preferred future. Clarify the issues and provide the champion with a date to come back to the board with the initiative plan.
- Spend time thinking, dreaming, discussing the future, and asking God for His direction and wisdom.

This kind of annual rhythm provides a regular touch point for intentional ministry evaluation and planning. The values, mission, preferred future, and ministry initiatives should be a central part of this annual retreat. Together, you can celebrate God's work among your people and plan your next steps. In addition, you will grow together as a leadership team and grow in the art of leading your flock into greater ministry effectiveness.

INTENTIONAL LEADERSHIP

Deeply intentional leadership, like the building of Prairie Ledge, results in ministries with the best opportunity to yield significant results. Accidental leadership is more likely to yield random results—like the Winchester House. In general, the single most important factor that separates successful ministries from those that are not is intentionality. The discipline of leaders to develop transformational ministries is a game changer!

Intentional ministries realize they cannot do everything at once, but understanding the direction they are headed can help them move toward their preferred futures in a disciplined and intentional way. They are deeply committed to their mission, always live in sync with their chosen values, know where they are headed, and are intentional on an annual basis in getting there. How are you and your board doing in living out intentional leadership for your church?

H. I. MOMENT

On a scale of 1 to 5 (with 1 being unintentional and 5 being very intentional), how intentional are we about making decisions that move us toward a preferred future? _____(Share answers with other board members.)

Over the past several years, what was the most successful ministry initiative our church undertook and why?

What key ministry initiatives are we currently involved in?

What are the next two or three initiatives needed to move closer to our preferred future?

Do we as a leadership group (along with key staff members) take time annually to determine how to move toward our preferred future?

H. I. WRAP-UP: INITIATIVES

- Key ministry decisions (initiatives) are always based on your preferred future.
- Concentrate on a few key initiatives at a time: Less is more.
- Initiatives need a champion, a plan, and a timeline.
- Work on developing a healthy culture of accountability for results.
- Initiatives always include measurable results.
- Be flexible when situations change.
- Evaluate initiatives honestly when completed.
- Develop an annual rhythm.

Part Three

EMPOWERED LEADERS

empowered structures

healthy church leaders

Intentional leadership

maximum ministry results

Jesus designed the church to be the most missional, effective, and flexible organization on the face of the earth. Too often our governance structures and cultures make it the most institutional, ineffective, and inflexible organization on the face of the earth.

Chapter Eleven

BUILDING CULTURES OF EMPOWERMENT

"Frustration" is the Chicago tollway at rush hour — roughly defined as most of the day! Whoever designed this highway toll system that forces all cars to stop or slow down at a tollbooth every five miles is responsible for millions of wasted hours and unbelievable inefficiency. Not to mention lots of frustrated drivers. Every time I drive through I ask myself why one of the most sophisticated nations in the world cannot figure out how to manage its roads more effectively. "There has *got* to be a better way," I mutter.

That is the echo of thousands of church leaders who live with the frustration of numerous "tollbooths" in their congregational systems. In churches, a tollbooth is every place where someone must get permission, funding, or agreement to move ministry forward. Many congregations live with cultures every bit as frustrating and inefficient as the Chicago tollway. These systems come with a high cost: wasted time; lost ministry opportunities; and frustrated leaders, staff teams, and volunteers muttering, "There's got to be a better way."

There is.

Our churches must become cultures of empowerment if we are to be the people God called us to be. The third section of this book is all about developing cultures of empowerment in your congregation. It is about moving from a permission-withholding culture ("You cannot act without permission") to a permission-granting culture ("You are welcome to act within your sphere of responsibility without asking permission"). It is about unleashing and releasing leaders to lead, staff teams to act, and congregations to minister so the church is everything God made it to be. It is killing bureaucracy wherever we can and creating cultures of great ministry opportunity.

THE DYSFUNCTIONS OF BUREAUCRACY AND CONTROL

I would argue that two defining characteristics of church cultures are bureaucracy and control. These are often fueled by a third characteristic: mistrust. Together, these three dysfunctions disempower at every level, preventing church cultures from freely carrying out responsibility. Let's take an inventory of commonly expressed frustrations.

As I've spoken with church leaders (both inside and outside the United States), I frequently hear frustration that church members desire a say in all decisions. While it is legitimate for congregations to have a say in some things, the desire by many congregations to have all decisions brought to them has the threefold result of cumbersome decision-making, disempowerment of leaders (why have them, if everything is decided by the congregation?), and staff frustration over the inability to get things done.

Another frustration surfaces when we consider the governance structures we use, many of which are bureaucratic nightmares where ministry decisions are spread across multiple groups. One group is responsible for overall direction of the church, another for the budget (guess who really has the directional power), and then subgroups must negotiate key decisions with both of these groups.

Then there are the frequent frustrations expressed by pastors who feel micromanaged and controlled by boards. In some cases, the senior pastor has almost no authority to make decisions. In these cultures, the pastor becomes the mere hireling of the board—or constant conflict results. Neither is healthy.

Staff teams may feel frustrated that they do not have the freedom to manage the daily aspects of ministry without the board being involved. What you end up with are two entities, staff and board, both weighing in on decisions. This is particularly disempowering to staff members, who are often highly qualified and in tune with the day-to-day needs of the church yet find someone always looking over their shoulders, questioning their decisions.

Sometimes the controlling entity for staff members is not the board but the senior pastor, who has not released responsibility and authority to them and has a need to control everything. Where this happens, good people chafe, leading to high staff turnover and poor ministry outcomes.

Come to think of it, the Chicago tollways might be more efficient than many congregations! If you think I exaggerate, I would invite you on any number of church consultations where these frustrations regularly surface.

I do not intend to convey that the bureaucracy and control are always deliberate. While the frustration is real, the causes are often unintentional. Many times congregations seek to control boards because they perceive that is their "job" in the congregational structure. Sometimes boards and staff teams frustrate one another because they lack clarity over who is responsible for what. When a governance structure causes frustration, it's usually not because it was written to control (though I have seen some that were). Rather, these structures were put into place when the congregation was small and only became cumbersome as the church grew. Many senior pastors micromanage staff members not out of a desire to control but because they haven't been trained in how to establish clear parameters and release staff to do their work. Likewise, when staff teams do not develop, empower, and release the congregation, it is not usually out of animosity. That "control" most often arises because leaders do not understand how to release people into ministry while maintaining philosophical ministry alignment throughout the church.

Whether intentional or not, these dysfunctions hinder the health of the church, the happiness factor of those involved, and the ministry effectiveness. Is it any wonder so many churches find themselves ineffective, with frustrated staff members, board members, and volunteers who simply leave for other churches where they are empowered to minister? The net loss to ministry is huge.

H. I. MOMENT

Which of these or other frustrations are true in your situation?

THE DYSFUNCTION OF MISTRUST

What lies behind the control that characterizes so many of our ministries? Often it is the third characteristic that leads to disempowerment: the dysfunction of mistrust—whether subtle or overt. Congregations mistrust boards, so they insist that all or most decisions come back to them. Boards mistrust senior pastors, so they don't release them to lead. Boards mistrust staff members, so they micromanage their work, In turn, because they are not empowered, entire staff teams mistrust boards and feel that boards are "into" power. This culture of control and mistrust bleeds into how staff members work with volunteers, not fully releasing them into ministry but needing to "manage" them ("After all, we are trained and they are not").

Mistrust breeds control. Control feeds mistrust. It is an unhealthy cycle.

Most likely, every leader or staff member reading this book can point to a situation where mistrust created frustration or, worse, deep conflict. Sometimes the root of the mistrust is plain: sinful attitudes. Often, however, it is the result of poor governance, management, or communication practices. While unintentional, they nonetheless resulted in pain.

H. I. MOMENT

In what areas of your church have there been — or are there currently — issues of mistrust? Take a moment and identify what you believe to be the root causes of this mistrust.

- _____
- _____
- _____
- _____

JESUS AND EMPOWERMENT

When we study Jesus' life and ministry, we see neither control, bureaucracy, nor mistrust. Instead, His ministry reveals an amazing bias toward empowering and releasing others. After giving instructions, Jesus sent out His disciples to minister—without Him. Beyond the twelve disciples, He sent out other groups to act on His behalf, such as the seventy-two (see Luke 10:1-24). Never do we see Jesus trying to control people in ministry. That does not mean He had no parameters: Jesus gave specific instructions and then debriefed and taught afterward.

Jesus knew that sinful culture loves to control and is slow to unleash. When the mother of two of Jesus' disciples asked that her sons be granted the honor of sitting to the left and right of Him in heaven, Jesus replied, "You know that the rulers of the Gentiles lord it over them, and their high officials exercise authority over them." He then went on to describe that leaders in His kingdom must lead differently: "Not so with you. Instead, whoever wants to become great among you must be your servant, and whoever wants to be first must be your slave—just as the Son of Man did not come to be served, but to serve, and to give His life as a ransom for many" (Matthew 20:25-28).

Jesus came to redeem mankind and establish His church, which is His visible presence on the earth. Before His ascension, Jesus tasked the church with evangelizing the world and making disciples until that moment when He returns to claim His bride. Jesus staked everything on the church, empowered by His Spirit.

Jesus took the biggest gamble of all time: He entrusted His church to His disciples. Think of that. He took His most precious possession and entrusted it to the likes of Mark and Peter and John and Matthew and you and me. He basically said, "Run with it, according to My instructions and in the power of My Spirit." Rather than keep ministry to Himself, He gave it away . . . and trusted us.

This is the point of Ephesians 4, where Paul wrote that Christ gave gifts to the church when He ascended into heaven: "It was he who gave some to be apostles, some to be prophets, some to be evangelists, and some to be pastors and teachers" (Ephesians 4:11). Christ gave these individuals His ministry of leading and equipping the church. He asked them, likewise, to give ministry away. He made them responsible to "prepare God's people for works of service, so that the body of Christ may be built up until we all reach unity in the faith and in the knowledge of the Son of God and become mature, attaining to the whole measure of the fullness of Christ" (Ephesians 4:12-13). The central focus of church leaders is to follow Christ's example and command as we develop, empower, and release people into meaningful, active ministry (that's the fifth leadership dimension we looked at in chapter 4).

Even knowing the frailties of men and women — that ministry would be done imperfectly and sometimes poorly — Jesus trusted them, empowered by His Spirit, to represent Him well, to build the church, and to reach a broken world with the gospel. This is not a picture of control but of empowerment. If Jesus was willing to risk giving His ministry away, we must be willing to risk along with Him.

H. I. BEST PRACTICE

Healthy congregations intentionally develop cultures of trust and practice giving ministry away. Healthy congregations trust and empower leaders, who trust and empower staff members, who trust and empower the congregation to do the work of ministry in all of its facets.

A close friend had a passion for reaching out to unsaved professionals who would not come to the average church service. He approached his church leaders and asked permission to start a once-a-month Saturday-evening event geared for this group. After much negotiation and discussion, he was finally granted permission.

More than three hundred people showed up on the first Saturday. Shortly thereafter, the leaders of the church informed my friend he could not continue. They weren't willing to give that kind of ministry away when it was not an official function of the church. It threatened them; they felt the need to step back in and regain control.

Eventually my buddy realized he was not going to be released within his church, so he did what so many find they must do: He started a new ministry that now numbers more than seven thousand in weekend attendance, is the largest congregation in town, has a high degree of conversion growth, and is influencing ministries across the United States. While I rejoice at what God has done in this ministry, I grieve for the original congregation that would not empower him and give ministry away. Think of what it cost them. *Risk — church unleashed!*

Empowering and releasing for ministry pleases the heart of God because that is who He is, what He did, and what He has asked us to do. Controlling and holding ministry tightly hurts God's heart, disempowers God's people, and compromises the ministry of the church.

H. I. MOMENT

Would you characterize your church culture as one of great trust and empowerment or one of command and control?

Complete this thought and then discuss it with the board (or staff team): "When I find it hard to empower others, it is because . . ."

- _____
- _____
- _____
- _____

H. I. MOMENT FOR CHURCH STAFF

Where do you feel empowered and where do you feel disempowered in your current church structure?

WHY IT MATTERS

What happens when we release people to use their full gifting, when we trust people and the Holy Spirit? The New Testament is clear that maturity comes to individuals and to congregations when they are released into meaningful ministry. Paul said,

> Then we will no longer be infants, tossed back and forth by the waves, and blown here and there by every wind of teaching and by the cunning and craftiness of men in their deceitful scheming. Instead, speaking the truth in love, we will in all things grow up into him who is the Head, that is, Christ. From him the whole body, joined and held together by every supporting ligament, grows and builds itself up in love, as each part does its work. (Ephesians 4:14-16)

What happens? Our congregations become mature; our people are productive for the kingdom; and love prevails. Mistrust and control breed conflict, bickering, and smallness of ministry. Trust and empowerment get people into the game of meaningful ministry. They bring energy, unity, enthusiasm for what God is doing, and kingdom fruit. Which would you rather have?

The tollway in Chicago is not quite as painful for those who purchase electronic passes. They can cruise through without stopping. The goal of building cultures of empowerment is to allow ministry in the local church to move quickly and effectively, within agreed-upon parameters and with as few tollbooths as possible — to move from tollbooths to passes for the sake of the mission Jesus left His church.

By gifting every believer with significant gifts to be used for His kingdom, Christ designed the church to be the most empowered institution on the face of the earth. In the next three chapters, we will illustrate how leaders can create cultures of maximum freedom and empowerment within agreed-upon boundaries. Are you ready to go there?

H. I. MOMENT

On a scale of 1 to 5, with 5 being a fully empowered culture and 1 being a nonempowered culture, where would you rate your church? _____ Share your answers with one another. How do you think staff members would answer the question?

Do your governance structures tend to release and empower or control and disempower? Can you give examples for either answer?

What is your response to the theology of Ephesians 4 that the job of leaders and staff members is to give ministry away rather than control it?

H. I. WRAP-UP: CULTURES OF EMPOWERMENT

- Cultures of bureaucracy and control hinder effective ministry and discourage good leaders and staff members.
- Mistrust is a dysfunction of the church.
- Jesus practiced empowerment in His ministry rather than control.
- Jesus gave ministry away to leaders and staff members, and Paul commands us to give ministry away to others.
- Healthy congregations intentionally develop cultures of trust and empowerment at every level.

Chapter Twelve

BIG ROCKS, PEBBLES, AND SAND

One of the most frustrating aspects of church leadership is the tendency of boards to deal with minutiae rather than the significant matters. This chapter will help leaders understand how to distinguish between "big rocks" (issues that boards must deal with) and "pebbles" or "sand" (issues that can be delegated to others). If boards properly distinguish between rocks, pebbles, and sand, they can grow in their ability to lead into the future rather than manage the status quo.

Big rocks drive ministry forward, affect the whole church, concern spiritual health, and relate to doing ministry more effectively (future focused). Big rocks are:

- Values, the nonnegotiables that define "who we are"
- Mission, the reason for the church's existence
- Vision, where God desires the church to go
- Ministry initiatives that move the church toward vision fulfillment
- Six-dimensional leadership (ensuring oversight over spiritual power; teaching; protecting; care; developing, empowering, and releasing; and leading)
- Policies that guide ministries
- Steps that ensure church health

failure—thinking that all there is is small stuff.

Pebbles and sand are the smaller issues that affect church life:

- Day-to-day management questions
- Staff supervision
- The development of specific ministry plans or strategies
- Details of church life that can be delegated to others

When boards consider their work, there are always more rocks than they can deal with in the time available. But here is the good news: Leadership boards are not supposed to handle every rock, only the *big* ones. In a pile of rocks of different sizes, the smaller rocks, pebbles, and grains of sand sift to the bottom. Boards are called to deal with the large rocks and allow all smaller rocks to filter down to lower levels of church management. The pebbles are important; someone has to deal with them, but they are not the task for boards.

Most of us are thinking, *I like that idea, but how do we ensure we are doing the work of boards and not getting bogged down in the sand?* Effective boards carefully determine their agendas and prioritize their work, rather than allow the whole pile to distract them from true leadership.

One of the ways to start is by understanding the differing responsibilities of staff teams and boards.

DIFFERING TEAMS, DIFFERING ROLES

A core distinction between the roles of a church's staff and its board is that *day-to-day management* falls to staff members or key volunteers, while *governance* — the establishment of policy and direction — falls to the church board. As a basic rule, everything related to management that can be delegated to a staff team ought to be.

A smaller church does not have a great need to talk about differing roles. In a church of 150 or fewer, and in any church with a only one or two staff members, this distinction is fuzzy. After all, with such a small staff, board members often function as both board members and volunteer staff members in other contexts.

Everything changes, however, as a church grows larger! A fundamental principle seen throughout this book is that a church does not only grow numerically, it changes — causing an ongoing need for governance systems to reflect its current size. The larger the church, the more important it is to be clear on the division of responsibilities. Both staff teams and boards become frustrated with one another in the absence of clarity, assuming (many times correctly) that the other is encroaching on their responsibilities. In a church of eight hundred-plus, few management decisions should come to a board.

Also different governate have different expectations

It is not unusual for some board members to resist this delegation of responsibility, either because they feel they could do it better or because they don't understand role differences between boards and staff.

to involunt

In the absence of delegation, three things can happen. First, a (not always subtle) tug-of-war commences between staff and board over "who's on first and who's on second." Second, you may lose good staff members; they will not stay forever if they are not empowered to do what they are trained to do. Finally, staff members may passively allow the board to call the plays, which seems to work for a while. But by the time a church hits the three-hundred mark, a board cannot call the day-to-day plays effectively. By then, however, staff members have become used to the board doing management, and they may be reluctant to do so themselves. After all, the board will probably second-guess their decisions.

This caused a real crisis in one church where I consulted. The board believed the senior pastor was unable to supervise his staff and that team members were incompetent, so the board maintained management control. After ten years of the board calling the plays, the senior pastor didn't try very hard to supervise, and the staff simply did what the board asked. The result was a fair amount of frustration in an otherwise healthy, growing church. The issue was ultimately resolved when board members stepped away from management; staff members took responsibility for that work; and the senior pastor received coaching in management and leadership. Without intervention, the situation could easily have led to the senior pastor leaving.

Whereas we hired Walt.

When boards insist on managing day-to-day ministry, they violate good governance *and* neglect the big rocks that define their true work.

PRINCIPLES FOR EFFECTIVE BOARD WORK

There are several practical principles you can apply to keep your board focused on the big matters.

Concentrate on direction and policies—not management. As we've seen, full-time staff members or volunteers—not the board—should manage day-to-day matters of church life. Before management decisions are taken up at the board level, ask, "Who should be empowered to deal with these kinds of questions? Do we need to develop a policy so others can make the call in the future?" For instance, many boards find themselves approving volunteers who teach Sunday school or do various ministries. While these kinds of topics might come to the board for quality-control purposes, this level of detail takes up valuable time. Rather than getting involved on a case-by-case basis, the board should develop policies by which others can make decisions. For ministry volunteers, the board can delineate who is eligible to serve in various ministries and then allow staff members or volunteer leaders to approve participation.

Spend more time on future plans than present issues. Leaders think ahead of the congregation. If you are spending the majority of your board time on day-to-day questions, you are probably deep into management rather than spiritual health, values, mission, vision, or ministry initiatives. To determine your present/future balance, keep track of the time you spend in a month on current matters compared to future plans and opportunities.

A common practice that traps leadership boards in the present is listening to long reports about ministries that have already taken place. This is a poor use of board time. Most reports ought to come to the board before board meetings via e-mail—a practice that can save up to an hour of precious board time. Yes, there are present issues that boards must deal with, but if you are spending more time on past reports or current ministry items than on future opportunities, your board priorities are reversed.

Our problems —
Everybody has an opinion.
Everybody's verbal...

BIG ROCKS, PEBBLES, AND SAND

Build meetings around big points, not small ones. Some topics belong with the board; many agenda items that come to boards do not. When building meeting agendas, ask, "Is this a big rock or a small rock—can others can deal with it, or does it need board discussion?" Whoever chairs your meetings must be given authority to build meaningful agendas and defer lesser matters to others. Often, people bring a discussion question to the board or to a board member rather than taking it to the person actually responsible for a ministry—a violation of good governance and of healthy relationships. As a board chair for many years, I would routinely ask people who had issues for the board if they had first taken them to the appropriate individuals. Inevitably, the answer was no.

Sometimes, it's a board member who adds inappropriate topics to the agenda. But just because someone is on the board does not mean he or she has the right to bring pet issues for discussion. Certainly, leadership brings opportunity to address many topics, but even board members must discipline themselves to remember that a leadership board does not exist to solve the pebble-sized problems. A board exists to provide good leadership and to empower others.

Craft your meeting agendas. To ensure you spend the majority of your time on big rocks, place the most important items first on the board-meeting agenda—and always use a written agenda. A carefully written agenda provides a road map for board work and encourages the discipline to place big rocks first and pebbles later. If your time runs out before you get to the less-important items, delegate them to someone else. Often they are not truly board-level items in the first place.

Delegate regularly. Here is a general rule: Don't do anything as a board that others could do. We give staff members and volunteers far too little credit for what they are capable of. If an item comes up that others can figure out, either delegate it outright or, if necessary, ask someone to come up with a proposal and bring it back to the board.

Refine, don't design. Boards are not good places to design programs or figure out complex problems. When a plan is needed, such as for issues related to human resources, compensation, or church conflict, it is far better to delegate the task to a working group. Ask two or three individuals with the necessary expertise to return to the board with a recommendation for approval or tweaking. It is much easier for a board to respond to a recommendation than to craft one up front. Staff teams (or volunteers) design; boards refine.

H. I. BEST PRACTICE

If the board has delegated an issue to a working group, don't redo its work. You may tweak the work or ask the group to revise, but don't micromanage the task. If you do, you are no longer delegating but are designing by committee — as well as negating the recommendations of the working team.

Stay within agreed-upon time parameters. When you ask leaders to serve, you are asking them for their most precious commodity: their time. Your board members should be able to expect that meetings will start—and stop—on time. If your meetings regularly run longer than two and a half hours, you are probably not exercising discipline in the conduct of your meetings or the size of the rocks you are dealing with. Or you may be attempting management or design at the board level. Empower your board chair (working with the senior pastor) to craft the board agenda and keep your meetings on task. Where there is gridlock or a lack of consensus, allow the chair to table the issue for future meetings.

Meet twice a month: once for business and once for prayer.[1] One of your gatherings ought to be a business meeting where decisions are made. I strongly recommend that your second monthly meeting be a "shepherding" meeting where no business is conducted. This is a time to pray for one another and for your church, to study Scripture and read chosen books together, and to dream about the future.

With rare exceptions, church business should be able to be accomplished in twelve meetings per year. A decision to spend the other half of your meetings in prayer and Scripture indicates a strong desire to keep the spiritual temperature of the board at a high level so they can model Six-Dimensional Leadership. Boards that have adopted shepherding meetings have experienced significant spiritual growth and greater unity in making decisions. They also have time to talk about future ministry without immediate pressure to make a decision.

A shepherding meeting reminds us monthly that we serve as under-shepherds to Christ, Head of the church. It is His agenda and will that we humbly seek. We cannot and should not try to lead His church without His power.

Agree on principles of decision-making. The genius of shared leadership is that a group of gifted people can accomplish more, and do it more effectively, than any individual — *if* their relationships embody mutual respect, love, and open engagement. Healthy boards can engage in robust dialogue[2] that results in creative solutions.

Boards often make one of three mistakes: (1) they don't engage in creative conflict due to conflict avoidance; (2) they engage in healthy conflict but aren't able to resolve it, leading to difficulty coming to a decision; or (3) they allow one or two board members to create and perpetuate conflict that holds the rest of the board hostage and unable to move forward.

Healthy boards invite honest conversation and even strong disagreements. However, they also agree to some basic rules of decision-making:

- A common question is whether to insist on unanimous decisions or to look for consensus. I would recommend boards work for unanimity but adopt consensus over unanimity as a practice. This prevents any one board member from stalling ministry decisions.
- All viewpoints are invited *inside* board discussions. But when healthy boards make a decision (even if not unanimous), they all agree to support that decision and present a united front *outside* the boardroom. Unless there is a significant moral issue at stake, board members who publicly disagree with board decisions are violating basic governance principles.
- Healthy rules for decision-making also include the policy that whatever the differences, board members will never violate one another by unkind words or poor attitudes. Differences of

opinion need not become personal; if they do, short accounts must be kept.

- Finally, a spirit of humility must pervade discussions, especially on potentially divisive questions. If Jesus could humble Himself and become one of us, we can humble ourselves to one another in His name. Those who cannot humble their views to the views of others should absolutely not be in church leadership.

Again, I want to recommend the adoption of the board covenant found in chapter 5. If you walk away from this book with just one concept, I pray that it would be this: *Healthy relationships on leadership boards matter*—to your spiritual life, to the spiritual life of your board, and to the spiritual life of the congregation you serve.

Whatever you need to do to resolve personal issues or to bring greater health to board relationships, I plead with you to do so. Remember, your church will likely not rise above its leaders. Establish your board rules for healthy, creative dialogue. Commit yourselves to live by those rules and graciously call one another to account when the rules are violated.

Practice cascading information.[3] A common frustration I hear when working with church staff is that they don't know what the board is up to. The impact of board decisions extends down through the life of the church, particularly to staff members and ministry volunteers. In addition, people's trust in their leaders correlates directly with their knowledge of what those leaders are doing. The more people know, the more they will trust, and the more they will be in alignment with their leaders.

Because of this, the final item that should be standard on every board business-meeting agenda is "cascading information": *What do we need to communicate about what we discussed or decided?*

Then, at the next staff meeting—where cascading information also appears as a regular agenda item—the senior pastor should convey those pertinent items from board meetings. Even if the information does not directly affect others now, the process breeds trust and helps staff members stay on the same page with leadership.

In a larger congregation with more leadership layers, staff meetings should continue the process of identifying cascading information to be communicated to the next level of staff or volunteers. This process continues in all ministry-team meetings until the information has cascaded through all levels.

Communicate board work to your congregation. A congregation's trust in its leadership is essential for a healthy church. Too often, work of a church board is shrouded in secrecy or mystery. While some issues must remain confidential, most work should regularly be communicated to the congregation.

The congregation does not usually need to know about the pebbles, but it does need to know about the big rocks. In fact, good communication regarding church values, mission, direction, and ministry initiatives helps educate the congregation as to who you are, why the church exists, where you are going, and how you intend to get there. As a general rule, you cannot overcommunicate these issues. The more you communicate, the more the congregation as a whole adopts these values and directional decisions as its own.

Most churches have congregational meetings that are used as forums for this communication, yet leaders are often frustrated by low attendance. Sometimes, these meetings center on reports of what has already happened in church life. In that case, should we be surprised if people do not attend? But there can be entirely different reasons for low attendance. Recently, I was called in to help explain major bylaw and governance changes to a congregation of more than two thousand. I spoke for five minutes in the Sunday-morning services and then spoke at greater length to a congregational "town meeting" that evening. Out of this large congregation, only about one hundred people came to the evening meeting. Why? Several reasons: The church was healthy; the congregation understood you do leadership differently as a large church; leadership had adequately communicated the changes; and people trusted their leaders to do the right thing! At a later meeting, the bylaw changes passed by an overwhelming majority.

If people don't attend your business meetings—for whatever

reason—should you eliminate those meetings? Not necessarily, but let me raise two thoughts. First, if your meetings are quarterly, you might want to consider meeting less often. Second—and here is the major suggestion—don't call them "business meetings" or "congregational meetings" but "vision nights" (or some equivalent). Use the meetings to communicate values and vision for the future ("new" news) rather than reports from the past ("old" news).

These are great opportunities to inform, motivate, and cast vision about what the church could be and the impact it could make for the kingdom of God. In fact, the meetings should be so well planned and so exciting that those who constitute the core of your ministry don't want to miss. (Offering great food and something fun doesn't hurt either!)

Even at annual meetings, where your bylaws may require you to elect leaders and approve budgets, make the business portion short and the vision portion the predominant piece of your meeting. Use your business meeting to communicate vision.

SORTING THE ROCKS AND PEBBLES

No matter what your size, be clear on the principle that "staff teams design and boards refine." Boards do the work of direction, policy, and spiritual oversight; staff members manage day-to-day decisions and ministry. In a large church, these roles are absolute; in a midsize church, fairly so; in a small church, more fuzzy.

Every year in their evaluation of themselves and church ministry, boards should ask, "Are there additional areas of management we can delegate to staff members?" Evaluating whether small rocks should fall to other levels allows the board to concentrate on leadership and empowers others to manage. The more you empower your staff members (or volunteers), the more effective they—and you—will be.

H. I. MOMENT

How well are we doing as a board in concentrating on big rocks? What keeps us from delegating smaller rocks and pebbles?

What percentage of our time in board meetings is spent dealing with the status quo or the past, compared with planning for the future?

Do we delegate ministry or program-design specifics to staff teams or a working group, or do we attempt to plan as a board?

Are there specific changes we can make to our meetings to accomplish more? If so, what are they?

- _____
- _____
- _____
- _____

How can we empower our board chair to help make these changes as he or she sets the meeting agenda?

H. I. WRAP-UP: PRACTICES OF EFFECTIVE BOARDS

- Understand differing roles of boards and staff.
- Concentrate on direction, spiritual health, and policies, not management.
- Spend more time on future plans than present issues.
- Build agendas around big points, not small ones.
- Craft your meeting agendas.
- Delegate regularly.
- Refine, don't design.
- Stay within agreed-upon time parameters.
- Meet twice a month: once for business and once for prayer.
- Agree on principles of decision-making.
- Practice cascading information.
- Communicate board work to your congregation.

Chapter Thirteen

STRUCTURE MATTERS

Remember that Chicago tollway full of starts and stops? We defined your church's tollbooths as every place someone must get permission, funding, or agreement to move ministry forward. These tollbooths, if they exist, are usually embedded in your governance structure — the bylaws and constitution that spell out procedures to be followed and committees to be formed.

While church governance may seem an arcane topic, structures *do* matter because they either serve or hinder our mission. My experience in working with churches is that the vast majority of our governance models are controlling (and deeply frustrating to leaders) rather than empowering. As such, they prevent the church from being nearly as effective as it could and should be.

In a recent consultation, an executive pastor of a church of five hundred told me a funny story. He needed to deal with some changes to the nursery ministry. When he asked around to find out whom the nursery folks were accountable to, nobody really knew (tollbooth). He went to the elders to explain the changes (tollbooth), then to the finance committee for funding (tollbooth), and finally to the "general board" to explain again (tollbooth) before he could finally accomplish the relatively minor changes.

Now if we believe mission is more important than structure and that structure ought to serve mission, these kinds of tollbooths would be unacceptable. But for some inexplicable (to me) reason, church bylaws (and therefore our governance systems) are often considered more sacred

*Our tollbooths were very real,
but not written down*

than Scripture! If you doubt that, think of some of the objections you face when you try to change them. Yet the early church clearly flexed their structures as the needs of the church changed. Deacons, for instance, were added early on to deal with issues that the elders no longer had time to handle. As the church grew, senior leaders started to delegate major ministry issues to others. This has continued to the point where, today, many congregations have multiple committees or boards that are never mentioned in the New Testament.

My point is that there is nothing sacred about the leadership structures of most churches. Governance structures, apart from what is clearly prescribed in the New Testament, are simply tools that should empower people and facilitate ministry.

Therefore, we should understand the origins of our church structures, how our cultural and theological understandings impact our views of structure, and principles that lead to healthy governance structures. And we must be willing to change our structures so that they support and serve our missions.

IN THE BEGINNING . . .

Governance systems are usually put in place when a church is young and often small. Here is what leaders need to understand about small churches (150 or fewer): They are like families. Families make decisions by consensus rather than through formal processes. Every year my family decides how we will spend our vacation time. We don't have a formal process of options or votes; we talk around the dinner table until the four of us come to agreement about our summer.

This is not unlike small congregations. The most obvious characteristics of a small church is that people know each other and all voices can be heard. I grew up in a family of twelve. My folks would consider our opinions on issues that affected us all. That's what you do in a healthy family. My parents still made the final call, but they always brought us into the discussion.

Similarly, small churches develop ways to talk together as a family

before major decisions, even if the congregation is 1
issue. Some congregations develop leadership sys
numerous elected boards and committees—often wi
that must ratify decisions of those boards and commit
highest value in a "family system" is to decide by consᴗᴗᴗᴗ and hear all
voices. In fact, while it is wise to put healthy governance systems into
place from the start, you can do governance with almost any system in
a small church, precisely because it is a family.

The cracks in unhealthy systems begin to show as a church grows. If
your congregation designed its governance at an earlier stage, you might
be frustrated by a complex and convoluted system that no longer works
well. These governance systems are defined more by sociology (church
size) than theology (New Testament prescriptions for governance).
When I suggest to a church that it change its system to move toward
what I consider is a more biblical and healthy governance system, I hear
one common objection: the need for checks and balances. NO TRUST!

CHECKS AND BALANCES

"If a church only has one board, and if great authority is vested in this
board," I am asked, "where are the checks and balances to its power?"
That is a good question and one that goes to the heart of congregationalism, which we will discuss in a moment. But it also reveals that the
American church is driven more by its national polity than by biblical
theology.

The U.S. government was designed with a carefully worked-out
balance of authority so that no one government branch could exert
disproportionate power over the other two (at least in theory). The fram-
ers of the Constitution had a high-enough view of the depravity of man
and the potential abuse of power that they tried to design governance
structures that would limit power and its potential abuse.

Interestingly, the New Testament also provides for healthy leadership accountability, but in a different way. The New Testament always
speaks of a plurality of overseers or elders, groups that include the

ing pastor. Authority is never vested in an individual but in a group of leaders. In addition, strict qualifications exist for leaders, starting with character qualifications. Leaders are not at liberty to do as they please (see Six-Dimensional Leadership in chapters 3 and 4). Rather, they serve on Jesus' behalf as His "under-shepherds" and will give an account for the quality and faithfulness of their ministry. That is huge accountability! Leaders are never the ultimate head of the congregation. Jesus is.

What you never find in the New Testament are competing boards or groups that exist to balance power or check leadership. As we will see in a moment, the congregation itself has the ability to override decisions of leadership, but there is no biblical model or rationale in the New Testament for other checks and balances to the authority of the senior leadership.

Another inherent reality behind the U.S. system of government is a basic mistrust of people who hold authority or responsibility. This mistrust runs deep in our national psyche. Recently, I did a consultation for a church of two thousand in Madison, Wisconsin, that was changing its bylaws. The senior pastor offered some perspective on the culture surrounding his church: "In this community [Madison], there is huge mistrust of anyone in authority. Everyone here wants to be in on decisions because they don't trust leaders."

Unfortunately, those attitudes often carry over into our churches. But the church is not the local government, and healthy leaders in the church are to be trustworthy and followed. The writer of Hebrews went so far as to say, "Obey your leaders and submit to their authority. They keep watch over you as men who must give an account. Obey them so that their work will be a joy, not a burden, for that would be of no advantage to you" (13:17). The New Testament clearly vests the senior leadership of the church with authority and responsibility for which they are ultimately accountable to God. *Trusts the system, not the shepherds*

Ironically, a checks-and-balances system of church governance actively fosters mistrust. Checks and balances inherently imply we should question and limit one another. Meting out authority to different groups brings opportunity for misunderstanding at best; in the worst-case scenario, outright conflict ensues. In these systems, decisions not only must pass through tollbooths, you have the added frustration of dealing with mistrusting tollkeepers!

The church needs a renaissance of trust among its people — trust between staff members and boards, between boards and congregations, and between congregations and staff teams. We need to teach our people that trust is biblical. When trust is violated, we need to work hard to restore it. Mistrust of each other may reflect our society, but it does not reflect our theology.

Along with questions about checks and balances, when I suggest changes to governance systems, people also wonder about congregationalism.

HOW DOES CONGREGATIONALISM FIT?

Many reading this book lead churches that are congregational in polity. The essence of congregationalism is that all believers are filled with the Holy Spirit and make up the body of Christ, so in a local fellowship the congregation is the final authority under Christ. This means that no ecclesiastical hierarchy can tell the church what to do and that a congregation can, if necessary, override leaders' decisions. Congregationalism is rooted in a theological understanding of the independence of the local church and the priesthood of all believers.

Because this biblical concept can morph into some unbiblical forms, it is important to understand what congregationalism does not mean.

First, congregationalism does not mean everyone in the congregation has an equal voice. If everyone's voice were equal, the leaders' job would simply be to poll the congregation and take the church in whatever direction was indicated. The New Testament, however, places a high premium on strong leadership from spiritually motivated individuals vested with responsibility and authority. In fact, the New Testament has a higher view of leadership than many congregations do (which ought to give us pause).

The New Testament model shows we are to choose godly leaders who have the gifts, skills, and character to lead on behalf of Jesus in directions that are consistent with God's mission. While the congregation plays a major role in choosing or affirming leaders, these individuals are trusted to lead and given authority to lead. Those who insist all members of a congregation have an equal voice may be reflecting a belief about how government should function, but they are not reflecting the biblical model for local-church governance.

Second, congregationalism does not mean all members have a voice on all matters. Those who have the hardest time with this concept are the ones who remember when their church was small (under 150) and naturally made decisions by consensus. As a church grows and leaders take more responsibility for decision-making, you often hear the complaint, "We are not congregational any longer." While we need to understand and be sensitive to the genesis of that comment, it is not necessarily true. Congregationalism looks different in different-size churches. A church can bring many or few decisions to the congregation and still be congregational. Leadership pain comes when churches don't realize this and continue to bring numerous issues to the larger congregation, creating the biggest tollbooth of all: the need to receive sign-off at congregational meetings on all decisions. It no longer works.

Ultimately, if a congregation has a say in choosing its leaders and senior pastor; in changes to its bylaws, constitution, and annual budgets; and in the sale or purchase of property, it is congregational, as it has the ability to override its leaders by changing leaders or withholding permission on budgets.

When the church leadership groups I work with understand that they can develop biblical trust and maintain congregational authority, they are often ready to begin considering changes to their structure.

HEALTHY GOVERNANCE STRUCTURES

Any writing or revision of leadership structures should be based on tenets that define healthy governance structures. The following principles are consistent with good governance and biblical teaching, where Scripture speaks to the issue.

Create only one board. A church should have only one board or senior-leadership group, and that board should have authority to make leadership and directional decisions consistent with the responsibilities spelled out under Six-Dimensional Leadership.

As we have seen, some governance modules build in multiple elected boards or committees so that authority rests in multiple areas. Many congregations, for instance, have a leadership board and a separate trustee board or committee that must approve budgets and spending. Having consulted with many churches, I am convinced that, in addition to a desire for checks and balances, some church constitutions were created with deliberate ambiguity about who's in charge. In one congregation, an administrative board was responsible for leading the church, but the senior pastor answered to the deacon board. Whether by intention or accident, no one was clear as to which board was ultimately responsible, which meant that *no one* could be held ultimately responsible.

This type of ambiguity hurts the church: No one has the ability to act decisively, and no one can be held accountable. If the intention is to prevent any one group from wielding too much power, the ambiguity succeeds. But it also prevents leaders from leading and the church from moving forward. *Representationalism!*

Another ineffective yet typical model is that of one "general" board made up of all elected committees and boards of the church. Under this model, the members of several elected entities make up a larger (often fifteen- to thirty-member) board that must ratify decisions made by the separate committees. The result? *General* boards make *general* decisions that yield *general* results with *general* accountability. Another difficulty with this structure is that leaders from the subboards are often representing their particular constituency rather than providing leadership for the entire congregation.

If your congregation elects more than one group of leaders, I strongly recommend calling only one of them a board (or whatever term you use) and making it clear that all other entities are accountable to this leadership group. There should be no question about which group is ultimately responsible for the direction of the congregation. In addition, the categories of this board's responsibility should be equally clear: church direction, spiritual health, budgets, and financial oversight.

Clarify roles, responsibilities, authority, and accountability. Bylaws should be clear on where ultimate authority lies, what issues must come to the congregation for decisions, and how elected entities or individuals relate to the senior-leadership board. Ambiguity in these areas causes confusion, conflict, and frustration. *When the board did not "listen" to the Fin Com they were frustrated*

Consider the financial confusion that occurs in a church with a senior-leadership board and a financial committee of some sort. Who determines the budget, and who controls the spending? Often the finance committee will assume it has this authority. Yet the leadership board's directional decisions cannot be divorced from financial decisions. This is a common source of conflict and frustration under traditional governance structures. *In hx, lots of violations here*

Another common area that lacks clarity is staff accountability. In good governance, only one person reports to the board and the board is accountable for only one person: the senior pastor. All other staff members report to the senior pastor. (In a larger church, staff will report to other supervisors, who then report to a senior staff member.) Many (flawed) governance structures require associate staff to be accountable to the board *and* the senior pastor. This structure violates a key management principle: No employee should have more than one boss. Associate staff members can easily be caught in a bind between what board members want and what the senior pastor wants. To whom do they listen? In addition, managing people by committee is inefficient.

Practically, this means senior pastors must play a major role in hiring staff, since staff will report to them. In addition, senior pastors must be empowered to hold staff members accountable for performance and given authority to terminate employment. All too frequently, senior pastors are held responsible for the staff team's ministry but are not empowered to hire or fire, which places them in an impossible bind. Wise boards will provide counsel to a senior pastor but not assume responsibility for staff issues.

Agree that structure must serve mission. Governance structures have one function: To help the congregation fulfill the mission of the church. Bylaws serve the mission, not the other way around. All leadership structures must be designed to empower biblical and effective leadership, and any structure that does not do so ought to be modified. Most businesses would be in severe trouble (or facing bankruptcy) if they operated with the kinds of leadership structures churches allow. Yet the mission of the church is far more important than that of any corporation, and the results of our ministry are eternal. Make it clear to your congregation that you will make changes to your governance as necessary so you can remain effective in fulfilling your mission.

Keep your bylaws as simple and brief as possible. Bylaws should be sufficiently clear to specify your governance, provide accountability, and keep you legal. They should be sufficiently brief to allow you to flex within your governance structure. For instance, many church bylaws spell out all the subsidiary committees. Often, however, these committee needs are out of date within a few years. Instead of specifics, simply indicate *If we create SOPs, we must up date them regularly!* that the leadership group may appoint or terminate ministry teams as needed. If you are congregational, identify the issues the congregation must decide, and leave the rest to the discretion of your staff or senior-leadership board. As leaders, you can always decide to bring additional issues to the congregation for their approval or input, but keep the list in the bylaws as brief as possible.

Remember that for many people bylaws are considered infallible—sometimes as sacred as Scripture. It's easy to create a situation where you are hamstrung by poorly written and too-specific bylaws. People who want to limit the authority of elected leaders are not shy about using bylaws to do so. Therefore, be wise regarding how much you include in them. Put what you must into your bylaws, but no more than you must.

Elect as few people as possible beyond your leadership board. This principle goes against the practices of many churches, which put their governance systems into place when the church was small and wanted everyone to have "something to do." So they established multiple boards and

SP, elders, and ??

189

committees—all elected. I was recently in a church of three hundred with elected spots for some eighty people. Of course, they are hopelessly unable to find people to fill all those positions.

Why specify as few elected positions as possible beyond your leadership board? (You may be required by law to elect a financial secretary and treasurer or certain other offices.) The most fundamental reason is that your needs will change over time and with the size of your church. Your bylaws should outline that the senior-leadership board has the authority at any time to appoint ministry teams and to terminate them when they are not needed.

The second reason is that when a congregation must fill many elected slots, its focus moves from finding people who have appropriate gifting to simply finding warm bodies.

Finally, because congregational election implies "authority," more elected positions brings more opportunity for boards and committees to "do what is right in their own eyes" without regard for the direction of your senior board. This can create confusion, misunderstanding, or even outright conflict. A system where your senior board is elected and other ministry teams are appointed by them provides much clearer accountability.

Use ministry teams to accomplish ministry tasks. When I recommend to congregations that they elect as few people as possible and establish only one board, the inevitable question arises: "But how can we get everything done?" Great question! I bring up the other side of the issue: "Are all the committees you currently have allowing you to get ministry done?" Candidly, I think that Satan enjoys our committees and our slow decision-making, because if we spend more time in meetings, we spend less time making an impact on our world. Good governance structures should result in the empowerment of people in ministry opportunities and the elimination of bureaucracy.

Ministry teams are a wonderful way to do this. Ministry teams are groups of individuals with a passion and gifting for a particular ministry. The leader of the team is appointed or approved by the board (or staff team), and that leader builds a team to accomplish a specific ministry task. It may be a team to drive youth ministry. It could be a car-ministry team that fixes up used cars and makes them available to single moms. Or it may be a compassion team that meet needs of the disadvantaged. Ministry teams can also be appointed to help a leadership board with specific tasks. For example, many churches lack staff expertise in the area of human resources, yet HR issues are critically important and bring legal implications. A leadership board might appoint a small team of trained individuals who can help develop policies and procedures and advise the church on HR-related issues. Because the teams are not spelled out in your bylaws, you can expand or contract teams according to needs. And because they are not elected, you can fill the teams with people who have a passion for a particular ministry.

The leadership board can maintain a ministry-team handbook that spells out how teams are started, how they relate to the staff or board, what ministry plans are required of them, and any other policies the board deems helpful. The handbook is a working document that can be changed as needed by the leadership board.

Change governance to reflect your church size. One size does not fit all. Certain principles are consistent with good governance across all church sizes, but a church of three hundred is not the same as a church of six hundred. Remember: Churches don't only grow, they change. And they require different ways of doing things in order to remain effective. This is why Leith Anderson—an author and pastor of Wooddale Church in Eden Prairie, Minnesota—tells his congregation (half tongue in cheek, half serious) that they will change something in their bylaws every year, whether or not they need to. Help your congregation understand that you *will* make changes as needed to stay faithful to your mission and remain effective at different stages in your church life.

STRUCTURE MATTERS

As I write this, a blimp is circling my city. One thing about blimps: They are *slow*. Unless we tweak our governance periodically, what was once a "fighter airplane" leadership system bloats into a blimp, frustrating everyone but the legalists.

Is your current governance paradigm a blimp or a fighter jet — or at least a 747?

The example of a blimp-like poor governance system on page 193 shows a summary of what we've been talking about. The maze of arrows indicates where permission, funding, or agreement must be obtained before decisions can be made. Decisions must be made more than once and with different groups. There is a lack of clarity as to who has authority to make decisions. The general board is typically made up of representatives of the other boards and committees, often causing members to be more concerned about their particular ministry than the church as a whole. At best, the system is confusing and time-consuming; at worst, it creates conflict along with its inefficiency.

In a nimble, healthy governance system on page 194, clear areas of responsibility are assigned to the congregation, leadership board, staff team, and ministry teams. Whatever authority is not retained by bylaw for each level is delegated to the next level. This is a model where each level empowers the next rather than forcing the next to obtain permission before moving forward. Ministry teams can be multiplied as necessary and are staffed by people with appropriate gifts and passions. Not only does this model provide clear governance and clarity of responsibility, it also reflects the theology of Ephesians 4, where the goal is to equip and deploy members of the congregation consistent with their spiritual gifts.

A healthy church can operate with a poor governance model. A church can also follow a great model and be unhealthy. However, if we desire to remove roadblocks to effective ministry, empower leaders to lead as they have been charged by the Scriptures, and unleash the greatest number of people in meaningful ministry, then structure matters—a great deal.

A POOR GOVERNANCE SYSTEM

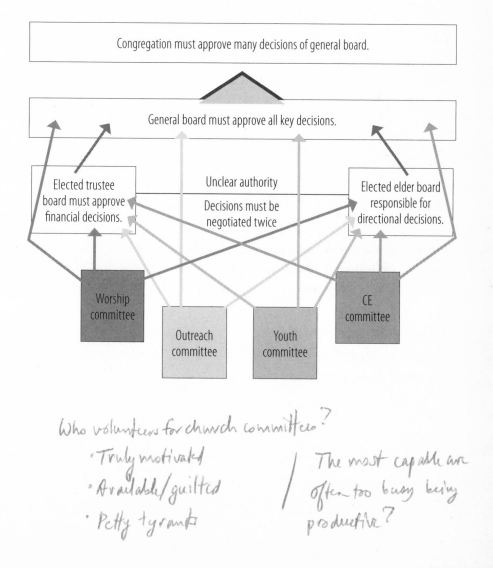

Congregation must approve many decisions of general board.

General board must approve all key decisions.

Elected trustee board must approve financial decisions.

Unclear authority

Decisions must be negotiated twice

Elected elder board responsible for directional decisions.

Worship committee

Outreach committee

Youth committee

CE committee

Who volunteers for church committees?
- *Truly motivated*
- *Available/guilted*
- *Petty tyrants*

The most capable are often too busy being productive?

A HEALTHY GOVERNANCE SYSTEM

Congregation elects leadership board and delegates all decisions to leaders apart from approving budgets, approving sale and purchase of property, calling of the senior pastor, and bylaw or constitutional changes.

The leadership board is responsible for congregational mission, direction, and policy; guards the values, mission, and preferred future; and approves ministry initiatives. The board delegates details and strategy to staff members.

The senior pastor serves on the leadership board.

The leadership board fulfills the responsibilities of Six-Dimensional Leadership

Staff members are responsible for day-to-day management and deciding how to implement vision approved by the leadership board. Staff members equip and deploy the congregation in ministries, based on passions and gifting.

Staff teams delegate day-to-day ministry details to ministry teams.

Teams are empowered to lead their ministries in line with church philosophy, with oversight by staff members.

Ministry teams operate within parameters determined by the leadership board.

| Ministry Team | Ministry Team | Ministry Team | Ministry Team | Ministry Team |

H. I. MOMENT

As it really is

Sketch a picture of your church governance, similar to the illustrations above, on a whiteboard. Then consider:

- Does our current structure help or hinder effective ministry?
- How does our church's structure compare to the illustration of effective governance structures?
- What structural changes would help us empower leaders and people to accomplish ministry?

H. I. WRAP-UP: PRINCIPLES FOR HEALTHY GOVERNANCE STRUCTURES

- Only one board
- Clarity on roles, responsibilities, authority, and accountability
- Structure serving the mission rather than mission serving the structure
- Simple and brief bylaws
- Minimum number of people elected beyond the leadership board
- Ministry teams used to accomplish ministry tasks
- Governance that reflects church size

Chapter Fourteen

NAVIGATING THE WHITEWATER OF CHANGE

Most likely by this point in our study, you have recognized issues you must deal with in your congregation. In fact, you probably started reading knowing that was the case—or at least suspecting so.

Now the question is, "Can you negotiate the change process?" Are you willing to wade in, knowing change brings risk? Introducing change to a system upsets the equilibrium. The resulting imbalance threatens many—even those in leadership. Pushback can occur. Loud voices can arise. *I was naive!*

If you have ever been whitewater rafting, you know the sense of instability you feel when leaving the peaceful water for the rapids. It seems you are at the mercy of the river; events are moving faster than you appreciate; you are getting wet. The sides of the raft rise or fall perilously, leaving your heart in your stomach—or your stomach in your mouth!

Those who like risk say, "Bring it on."

Those who don't like risk say, "Why did I ever agree to this? Get me out of here fast!"

Then from the rear of the raft, you hear the guide shouting instructions to pay attention, do as he says, and all will be well.

How does he know? He is an expert in whitewater. He has studied the river. He knows how to negotiate it safely. So far, he has never lost anyone (at least that's what he said). He told you before you started that if you just do as he says, you'll make it through. The risk-averse hope that to be true with all their hearts!

Change is often like whitewater rafting. Once you get into it, the situation can seem out of control; you start getting wet; it's hard to take in everything around you; loud voices are heard (and not just the guide's); and fellow rafters exert huge pressure to beach the raft, forget the change, and move back upstream to placid waters.

In fact, many leaders do just that. Fear forces them back to the past, to the calm, to the prior equilibrium. As a result, they miss the adventure of following the Holy Spirit to new waters of ministry.

This chapter is the last and perhaps the most critical one of the book. You can buy into everything you have read so far (I'll settle for a piece of that) only to allow fear to keep you from making necessary changes, whether in leadership dynamics, intentionality, or structures. If you balk now, you will have wasted your time. My goal in this chapter is to be the guide at the back of your raft, assuring you that if you approach the right change the right way, you will make it through the whitewater.

HOW PEOPLE REACT TO CHANGE

Make no mistake: There will be whitewater. We often wonder why there is such resistance to change; the answer lies in how people are made. In general, people are change-resistant rather than change-friendly. In his groundbreaking book *Diffusion of Innovations,* Everett M. Rogers studied reasons people adopt an innovation (change) or resist it. Rogers's book remains a seminal work on understanding how change occurs, why it meets resistance, and ways that this resistance can be overcome.

In part, Rogers studied public-health efforts to convince villagers in Peru and Egypt that they ought to boil water or use well water in order to reduce waterborne diseases. While some embraced the new ideas, the majority did not, even though they continued to become sick at a higher rate than those who did. Those who embraced innovation first were "early adopters" and became a guiding coalition who then influenced others. Normally it took some time before others changed their ways (early and late majority), and some never did (laggards). Resulting research showed these change patterns were not isolated to villages in Peru or Egypt but reflected how populations everywhere respond to change.

Rogers concluded that of people in a general population:

- 2.5 percent are innovators
- 13.5 percent are early adopters
- 34 percent are early majority
- 34 percent are late majority
- 16 percent are laggards[1]

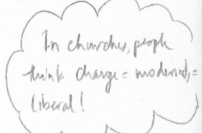

In churches, people think change = modernity = liberal!

Innovators are those who dream up new ways of doing things; early adopters respond quickly and adopt what they see as a good idea; early-majority folks are more deliberate in thinking through the innovation but, after consideration, will adapt; late-majority individuals will be skeptical of the innovation but eventually respond after seeing benefits; laggards are traditionalists who will probably never respond. For laggards, innovation is a bad thing.

Notice that only 16 percent can be labeled as "change-friendly" (innovators and early adopters); those who could be labeled as "change-cautious but open" are just over one third (early majority); which leaves 50 percent as those who are "change-skeptical" or "change-averse" (late majority and laggards). This explains why even the best ideas will be met with caution, skepticism, or negativity by the majority of any group (a reality innovators and early adopters don't understand).

To give a modern example of these categories, consider PDAs (personal digital assistants). Somewhere there were innovators who knew the world needed PDAs even while the rest of us were happy with our Franklin Planners. So they went about inventing devices such as my T-Mobile phone, which is a phone, planner, e-mail device, text messenger, and more.

As soon as these devices hit the market, early adopters like me knew they had to have one and found excuses to acquire one immediately *("How else can I be productive?")*. My father is somewhere in the early majority here. We would meet at the Nordstrom's coffee shop near my office, and he would ask to see mine. He would ask, "What all does it do?" Then he would add, "Do you think I need one?" It took a few years, but eventually he purchased two: one for himself and one for my mom.

The late majority are those who will decide they need a PDA just before PDAs go out of style in favor of the next thing innovators are even now working on. Laggards will never purchase a PDA and will always be content with their notebooks and pens.

Before I move on, let me make the point that there is nothing inherently good or bad about how people respond to change. A lot of what we perceive as obstinate behavior regarding change does not come from bad attitudes (although some does) but from how people are hard-wired.

The fact that more than 80 percent of a congregation is not in the innovator or early-adopter categories reveals the challenge leaders face as they help people move in new directions. Almost any major change is going to be greeted by whitewater, at least in the beginning.

H. I. MOMENT

Where do you fit in the change categories?

Discuss where board or staff members might fit.

Can you think of change situations within your congregation where, looking back, you can identify these different categories at work?

If you ever changed worship styles, how did these dynamics play out?

A WORD ABOUT LAGGARDS

Even leading with values doesn't mean that everyone will come on board with change; you may encounter ingrained resistance from the percentages who are late adopters—and especially the laggards. Laggards are found in every congregation. They are highly resistant to change (they are traditional—they like the way it is and always has been). My friend

Larry Osborne from North Coast Church in Vista, California, calls these folks "squeaky wheels." Laggards are usually a small minority, but they cause a whole lot of heartburn for leaders. They can have very loud voices and cannot be convinced.

In congregational meetings, they are the ones who speak the most and the loudest and are often the most negative. Because they are loud, others in the congregation may wrongly assume their view is widely held. And because loud voices threaten leaders, those leaders often spend an inordinate amount of time trying to placate the squeaky wheels. No matter how much time you spend trying to convince the squeaky wheels, you will not be successful. They are deeply change-resistant. You are wasting your time because they will always find something to squeak about. *I did!*

We would be much better off allowing squeaky wheels to squeak and working to convince others who can be moved than to waste precious time and energy trying to move people who will not be swayed.

H. I. BEST PRACTICE

Wise leaders are not swayed or threatened by squeaky wheels. Love them but find ways to marginalize their voices. They do not represent the majority of the congregation and cannot be allowed to slow down kingdom progress simply because they don't like change.

H. I. MOMENT

Who are the squeaky wheels in our congregation?

What has been our strategy for dealing with them?

Have we ever allowed their displeasure to compromise where we need to go as leaders or as a congregation?

H. I. BEST PRACTICE

Target the right people in the change process. Don't worry about the innovators or early adopters; once your rationale is explained, they will probably be on board. Also, don't try to convince the laggards; they won't get it. Just "manage" them to ensure their loud voices don't derail your process. Your critical targets are the early- and late-majority people, because they form the bulk of your constituents. When they are convinced the change is beneficial to the church's mission, they will likely agree to go with you.

VALUES TRUMP ALL

Link change to value expression

So how does a leader lay the groundwork for change among these various groups (excepting laggards)? Here is a key principle: A higher value trumps a lesser value. Most people are willing to change if they can be convinced the proposed change meets a value they hold more highly than the one disrupted by the change. (However, remember that their heart acceptance will be determined by where they are on the change curve.)

For instance, I have helped numerous congregations change their governance systems to reflect empowered cultures. Almost without exception, the late majority and laggards were negative when the change was first introduced. Even the early majority were cautious. However, when churches engage in a process that allows people's questions to be answered and they become convinced that a change in governance will help them reach more people for Christ (a high value of believers), most are willing to consider and adopt the changes. That's because they value reaching people for Christ more highly than they value maintaining their governance structure.

I know some of you read part two on mission, vision, and preferred future with a jaundiced attitude of "Why worry about this stuff?" Here is a major reason to care: When your congregation buys into the mission, vision, and preferred future, those elements become the cornerstone of your explanation for necessary changes. Even change-resistant people are already on board with what's really important, so they will be willing to consider alterations if you can show them how the change will result in better achieving your mission, vision, and preferred future.

I once consulted with a church that had a high value on everyone worshipping together in one service with one style of worship. When I challenged the leadership on this, they pushed back saying, "We'll never change this." I pointed out that this value conflicted with their value of reaching as many people with the gospel as they possibly could, since they were excluding anyone who did not feel at home in that worship style. That got their attention. Reaching people for Christ was a higher value than their value of everyone worshipping together. Today, this congregation offers choices of worship and has grown considerably.

RAPIDS AHEAD We did not do this

Before a whitewater-rafting trip, a good guide will sit everyone down and tell them what to expect. The reason is simple: Knowing what is in store lowers the anxiety level. At least rafters can say to themselves in the middle of the whitewater, *Our guide told us it would be this way.* Here are some realities of negotiating change, so you can say, "He told us it would be this way."

- You will face resistance. This is normal. Don't be anxious or discouraged when people don't instantly adopt your great ideas; that is how people are wired.
- A few loud voices will seek to shut down the change process. This is normal, too. Don't allow their voices to keep you from doing what you need to do. An exception would be individuals who you know have great wisdom, a history of being supportive (not squeaky wheels), and significant "coinage" with you and others. Not everyone's voice carries the same weight.
- Some people may threaten to leave the church. This is normal. The more intentionally you lead, the more resistance you will encounter; you are messing with the status quo. It is not unusual for people to leave when the congregation makes key directional

decisions. To cave in to threats is to compromise your church's kingdom impact because of a few loud voices. Don't cave!

- Leaders may suggest you revoke the changes, even though they previously agreed with the need. This is normal, although unfortunate. Change is about waves. Leaders who cannot live with waves are probably in the wrong place. True leaders don't retreat from something they believe to be right just because their proposed change brings pushback.
- The greater the change, the more uncomfortable you may feel. This is normal. It is hard to think calmly in the middle of white-water. Change produces anxiety in your congregation, which will cause *you* anxiety. Stay the course and work the process.
- You will get wet. This is normal. When the raft is bucking, water comes over the sides. When equilibrium shifts, people say sinful things and take shots at those who caused the waves. Respond in ways that lower the tension. And stay the course.

Did you see the theme here? "This is *normal*." So often when we are buffeted by rapids, we question our decision. We are tempted to retreat. We lose our nerve, thinking we must have really screwed up to be where we are. No! All of this is normal. Expect it and negotiate it with wisdom, patience, and low anxiety.

H. I. BEST PRACTICE

Recognize what is *normal* when negotiating the whitewater of change. Good leaders keep these realities in mind and are not deterred when they occur. Talk about them as a group before you enter the process; remind everyone it will not be smooth sailing.

H. I. MOMENT

Which of these normal reactions have we seen when we walked the congregation through change?

Faced with these reactions, when did our leadership or staff respond in healthy or unhealthy ways? Share examples.

CHARTING A HEALTHY CHANGE PROCESS

Okay, now that you know what to expect, let's chart the course of what a healthy change process looks like. Knowing that changes need to be made is half of the challenge. The other half is designing a process that is most likely to result in your desired conclusion. The key word here is *process*. When change goes wrong, it is usually connected to a process that is flawed or short-circuited.

Chances are good that after reading this book you may decide you need to tweak or change your governance system. Therefore, while the principles remain the same for any major change process, I am going to use governance change as the example of how a healthy process may work.

Prepare people for coming changes. The process starts by preparing people for change. People do not like surprises. Once the board knows you will begin a process of change (such as revising your bylaws or constitution), let people know what is coming and why. You are not communicating final decisions; you are paving the way to start the process.

Gather information. Other leaders have walked through changes like yours before. If you are a pastor, ask fellow pastors, "Who has successfully negotiated the change process we are attempting?" Then find out what they did right and what they would have done differently. Ask what "dumb tax" they paid that you can avoid. Ask how the change or ministry initiative helped them missionally. What you learn will not only provide you with valuable insight but will also give you credibility with the congregation because you have done your homework.

Wisely choose a working group. Whether you are considering bylaw changes, a building project, or a major ministry change, bring together a working group who will do the work that results in a draft proposal to the congregation at large. The better your working group, the better your chances of success with the congregation. You need them not only to provide good counsel but also to serve as a positive voice for the rest of the congregation. A "worst practice" here is to recruit representatives from every group in the congregation—even intentionally bringing in people opposed to the change. I have watched leaders do this in the interests of keeping the peace. It is naïve and does not work.

Also consider bringing in a consultant who can provide outside perspective. An outsider's perspective can be an advantage in congregational meetings where a consultant can ask questions or make observations that would be difficult for an insider to make.

Always tie your proposed changes to your values, mission, or preferred future. Whenever you talk about the change, always tie it to your values, mission, or preferred future. The discussion is not fundamentally about structure or programs; it is about mission fulfillment. The more you communicate this, the more people will get it.

Why would you consider changing your bylaws? You would do so because a governance structure that worked at one stage of your congregation's life no longer fits. What is sacred to the congregation is the mission, not the structure. Therefore, because the structure has become a hindrance to ministry effectiveness, you must find ways for the structure to serve the mission.

One guru on change processes, John Kotter, suggested that in order to get people's attention and convince them of the need for change, you must "create a crisis."[2] In congregations, the "crisis" is that not changing will compromise (or is already compromising) our ability to do what Christ has called us to do. Again, it is all about mission.

Recruit a guiding coalition. During any key change, you want a guiding coalition who will publicly and privately support the process.[3] This coalition certainly should include all board members and ministry-staff members. (If there are board members or staff members who are not publicly supportive, you have other issues to deal with.)

The coalition should also include people of positive influence in the church who can help the early- or late-adopting majority understand the need for change. In the example of bylaw changes, the most resistance often comes from long-standing members. They either helped create the original bylaws or are simply used to the way things are. If an influential person from their generation can positively represent the need for change, they may look at the process with greater openness.

This is not a lobbying exercise but recognition that people influence people and that every congregation includes key influencers. If these influencers understand where you are going and the reasons for moving there, they become voices of reason and encouragement to the rest of the congregation.

If you find your key influencers are opposed to your suggestions, you may want to do more groundwork before you move forward. After all, wise leaders are not going to propose something they think will not have the support it needs to succeed.

H. I. BEST PRACTICE

Before you propose major change, know that it is going to succeed — to the best of your ability. You can test the waters by sounding out those you need in the guiding coalition.

Provide ways the congregation can offer input. Providing a means for members to ask questions and give suggestions is especially important in a high-stakes change process. The more open leaders are perceived to be, the more likely that the congregation will be supportive of the process and outcome.

Congregational meetings are not always the best forum for such discussion — people are less willing to ask questions and share opinions in large meetings. The one group, however, that is rarely shy about their opinions are the squeaky wheels. Thus, in large settings you run the risk that squeaky wheels will monopolize the discussion or be the only voices that are heard, leading others to assume many feel the same way.

A good practice is to hold a series of smaller meetings where people can talk with those leading the process. This is less intimidating, provides a more personal atmosphere, keeps squeaky wheels from derailing change, opens up leaders to suggestions, and reduces the stakes of conflict that can be higher in larger meetings. Holding smaller meetings also means that when the time comes for a congregational meeting, it is not necessary to provide unlimited discussion time (which most people do not want anyway), since the congregation has had plenty of opportunity for input along the way.

A good way to offer these meetings is to let people know that a leader will be available for discussion after Sunday-morning services. In my experience, not a lot of people show up. This is indicative that, for the most part, people trust their leaders.

In these small settings, it is critical for leaders to be discussing a draft, not a final proposal, so congregants feel they can actually influence the final outcome. The leaders should be nonconfrontive toward those with an alternate agenda, tie the discussion back to missional issues, and thank people for their input. This does not mean leaders need to agree with all points of view. It does mean that they need to listen in a nonthreatening way to all points of view and thank people for their willingness to share.

Even modest adjustments leaders make as a result of these discussions mean a great deal, because they send a strong message that the leadership listened and is open to suggestions. These opportunities for discussion, if handled well, will also alert leaders to issues that may be circulating within the church that could have a negative impact on proposals. Understanding these dynamics gives leaders a chance to modify proposals or be ready to speak to the concerns.

Having listened, come up with a final proposal that is likely to succeed. Throughout this congregation-wide input process, issues may arise that cause leaders to modify ministry proposals. Be careful which hills you want to die on. If you can move 80 percent of the congregation in the desired direction but cannot reach the last 20 percent, that is still more desirable than having no one with you. You do not want to sacrifice leadership capital over issues that can be resolved later or that are not key.

We once changed the bylaws significantly at my church while I was serving as chair of the board. The one issue people kept resisting was our desire to change the quorum for business meetings from 50 percent (a terribly high bar today) to 25 percent. Knowing this was a sticking point, we removed that recommendation, got almost unanimous

NAVIGATING THE WHITEWATER OF CHANGE

approval on everything else, and achieved 95 percent of what we wanted. Remember, you can always come back and propose additional changes.

Overcommunicate with the congregation. Possibly the greatest failure of leaders during a change process is not communicating adequately with their congregations. This usually isn't intentional. Leaders know what is happening and therefore assume others do as well. In addition, when they have communicated once, they feel the job is done. They underestimate the number of times they must say the same thing to a group before a message is heard. Without adequate communication, leaders are seen as aloof, arrogant, unaccountable, and power hungry—all of which are probably far from the truth.

Trust for change is gained by three simple disciplines: being missional, communicating well, and listening. As you talk to the congregation, tie everything back to mission. If the change is about mission, then it is not about a leader's or staff team's agenda but God's agenda. That makes all the difference in the world to most people. Second, communicate constantly about what is happening, what the board is thinking, and why it is thinking what it is thinking. Again, always tie this back to mission. Third, as we've discussed, regularly listen to people and provide easy forums for them to meet with leaders. This builds trust—even if few people come.

When boards and staff teams are asked if they communicate enough, they usually answer, "Of course." When congregations are asked if boards and staff teams communicate enough, the answer is usually, "No." Even if it is an unfair perception, perception is reality.

Do everything you can to keep anxiety and conflict over possible changes low. As we have noted, anxiety over change often brings out the worst in people—much like weddings and funerals do in families. Whenever anxiety is present in a family system—and the congregation is a family system—one of the leader's jobs is to lower anxiety wherever possible.

Anxiety doesn't only occur at a congregational level. Leaders have a lot invested in major proposals they make, and it is normal for them to become defensive when people resist or even attack. Having been a pastor and having worked with scores of pastors, I find us to be the most susceptible to defensiveness. After all, we are giving our lives for our congregation ("Woe is me"); we have their best interests in mind; and our self-image is too often wrapped up in what people think and how they respond to us. My advice? We need to get over it. The best thing we can do is to separate ourselves from our plans, adopt an attitude of "nothing to prove and nothing to lose," and respond kindly to all, whether they are on the attack, are negative, or are our best supporter.

Good leaders are great at lowering anxiety and deflating conflict. Identify your leaders with that gift and use them in congregational meetings, large or small. Remember, shepherds put up with all the sheep, protect all the sheep, and feed all the sheep — even those that are a pain to get along with (and some are).

Do not neglect a prayer strategy for major ministry initiatives. However you can, mobilize the congregation to pray during times of transition or change. Our battle is "not against flesh and blood, but against the rulers, against the authorities, against the powers of this dark world and against the spiritual forces of evil in the heavenly realms" (Ephesians 6:12). If you are proposing change because it will give you a greater return on mission, know that the Evil One will oppose you at whatever level he needs to. The bolder your plans, the bolder his response. If Satan can bring division or encourage bad attitudes and sinful junk to surface, he will. Even something as mundane as changing your bylaws is reason enough for attack. Why? Because your changes will make your ministry more effective. Sorry, but he doesn't want that to happen.

Just as you make mission the *focus* of change, make prayer the *process* of change. After all, our ministry future is not about what we think; it is what God thinks! And prayer is the key to understanding what God thinks — both for the individual and for the church.

RELAX, PERSEVERE, AND LEAD BOLDLY

Change is not about us. Ministry advances are not about us. God has called us to lead boldly, and even more so when leading is not easy. Leaders need to be wise, to respect process and people, and to trust

God for the outcome. What will surprise us more often than not is that when we do change right, the vast majority of those we lead will respond positively—even when they are not innovators or early adapters. Why? Because they share our desire to see Christ honored and His kingdom expanded.

In most cases, the greatest fear of change is not in the congregation but in leaders. We fear a response that does not materialize if process, people, and mission are respected. We are cautious to the point of weakness in challenging the congregation to change. We are intimidated by the few when the majority wants to go with us. Time and time again, like a guide on a whitewater trip, I have encouraged reluctant leaders that if they would do the right thing in the right way, things would turn out okay. And they did.

As leaders, we act on behalf of Christ for His church. It is His church, not our church. He wants ministry effectiveness more than we do, and He will honor our desire to lead His congregations to green pastures.

There is nothing more exhilarating than to be part of a church-leadership team that is passionate about taking territory for Christ, has a plan for getting there, and is empowered by the congregation and its structures to make it happen. I hope that after working through this book, your board can operate this way—or will work through the process to get there.

There is much at stake in how we do church leadership. At stake is the health of our congregations, their impact in our communities and the world, the number of individuals we can introduce to Jesus and help grow into fully devoted followers, and even the unity and love of those we lead. All of these rest on the health, intentionality, and empowerment of godly leaders.

My prayer is that you will take seriously God's call to become what He wants leaders to be, to lead as He wants you to lead, and to trust Him for significant ministry fruit. As you do that, you will find your ministry deeply fulfilling and a joy.

H. I. MOMENT

Are there changes or ministry advances we ought to be working on with the congregation?

Are there any that are overdue, due to our fear of bringing change?

What fears surface when we think of walking the congregation through substantive change?

H. I. WRAP-UP: CHARTING A HEALTHY CHANGE PROCESS

- Prepare people for coming changes.
- Gather information.
- Wisely choose a working group.
- Always tie your process and proposed changes to your values, mission, or preferred future.
- Recruit a guiding coalition.
- Provide ways the congregation can offer input.
- Having listened, come up with a final proposal that is likely to succeed.
- Overcommunicate with the congregation.
- Do everything you can to keep anxiety and conflict over possible changes low.
- Do not neglect a prayer strategy for major ministry initiatives.
- Relax, persevere, and lead boldly.

POSTSCRIPT

I am not an innovator for the most part; I am an early, early adopter. Thus, what I have shared with you, I have learned the hard way — by doing it wrong; by walking through all manner of leadership experiences; by consulting; by watching and learning from others.

As you read this book, I hope you had some "aha" moments. Perhaps you also said in places, "That wasn't clear," or, "I don't agree with that." Or maybe you had insights that could strengthen this book for future editions.

Anything you would like to share, I would like to hear. Please feel free to contact me at tj@AddingtonConsulting.com with any comments, criticisms, or suggestions. Let's learn from one another.

T. J. Addington

NOTES

Chapter 4: Six-Dimensional Leadership, Part Two

1. George Barna, *The Second Coming of the Church* (Nashville: Word, 1998), 21. See www.barna.org for updated information.
2. Copyright 1995 Willow Creek Community Church Participating Membership Manual. Used with permission.
3. "Invite Them into the Kitchen," an interview with Andy Stanley, *Leadership* (Winter 2000), http://www.ctlibrary.com/le/2000/winter/1.22. html (accessed September 1, 2006).
4. Adapted with permission from Bill Hybels, *Courageous Leadership* (Grand Rapids, MI: Zondervan, 2002), 139–159.

Chapter 6: A Parable of Two Houses

1. Tom Clegg and Warren Bird, *Lost in America* (Loveland, CO: Group, 2001), 25–35.
2. Clegg and Bird, 29.
3. George Barna, *The Second Coming of the Church* (Nashville: Word, 1998), 6.

Chapter 7: Values: Determining the Nonnegotiables

1. http://www.tworiverschurch.org. Used with permission.
2. "Becoming a Heartland Participating Team Member." Heartland Community Church, Rockford, IL. Used with permission.
3. http://www.wooddale.org/guest_center/values.asp.

4. Bill Hybels, *Courageous Leadership* (Grand Rapids, MI: Zondervan, 2002), 80–85.

Chapter 8: Mission: Establishing Your True North

1. Tom Clegg and Warren Bird, *Lost in America* (Loveland, CO: Group, 2001), 29.

Chapter 12: Big Rocks, Pebbles, and Sand

1. I am indebted to pastor and author Larry W. Osborne for this insight. Larry has a chapter on "The Shepherding Meeting" in his excellent book *The Unity Factor: Developing a Healthy Church Leadership Team*, 3rd ed. (Vista, CA: Owl's Nest, 2001), chapter 7.
2. The concept of "robust dialogue" or "creative conflict" for healthy teams is well spelled out in Patrick Lencioni's book *The Five Dysfunctions of a Team: A Leadership Fable* (San Francisco: Jossey-Bass, 2002). This is a must-read for boards and staff teams.
3. Again, I am indebted to Patrick Lencioni in his book *The Five Dysfunctions of a Team* for this insight.

Chapter 14: Navigating the Whitewater of Change

1. Everett M. Rogers, *Diffusion of Innovations*, 5th ed. (Free Press: New York, 2003), 281.
2. John P. Kotter, *Leading Change* (Boston: Harvard Business School Press, 1996), 35–49.
3. I am indebted to John P. Kotter, *Leading Change*, for this insight.

ABOUT THE AUTHOR

T. J. ADDINGTON is a senior vice president of the Evangelical Free Church of America (EFCA), an organizational consultant, speaker, and author. He resides in Minnesota with his wife of thirty-three years and is the father of two children, Jon and Steven (Chip). In his spare time he enjoys reading, traveling, writing, and fly-fishing. He is the author of two other books, *Leading from the Sandbox: Develop, Empower, and Release High-Impact Ministry Teams* and *Live Like You Mean It*. T. J.'s passion is to see God's people be all that they can be.

More great titles from NavPress!

Leading from the Sandbox
T. J. Addington
978-1-60006-675-7

Learn how to develop, empower, and release high-impact ministry teams within the church to go out into the world.

Live Like You Mean It
T. J. Addington
978-1-60006-673-3

Author T. J. Addington helps you think deeply about the most important issues of life, clarify their purpose, live intentionally, learn to play to their strengths, and make the most of the rest of your life.

Discovering the Bible
Gordon L. Addington
978-1-61521-269-9

Take a journey through the Bible in one year. In *Discovering the Bible*, Gordon Addington, gives you insightful notes and the historical background for each day's reading. See how God unfolds His amazing plan of redemption throughout the entire Bible. Leader's guide included on CD.

To order copies, call NavPress at 1-800-366-7788 or log on to www.navpress.com.

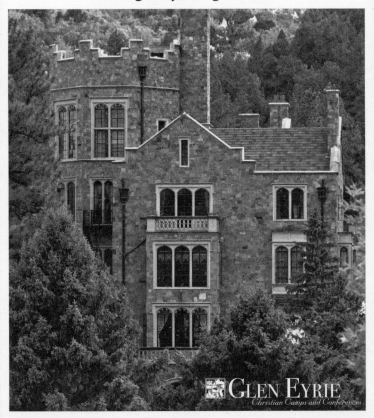